Michael LaFosse's
Origami
Butterflies

Elegant Designs from a Master Folder

By **Michael G. LaFosse** and **Richard L. Alexander**

TUTTLE Publishing

Tokyo | Rutland, Vermont | Singapore

Dedication

Origami, or paper folding, has been a decorative craft for hundreds of years, but only recently has it been recognized as a creative, expressive art. In only the last few decades, a vibrant international community of origami artists has flourished, thanks to the help from selfless artists, authors, and origami ambassadors. Michael LaFosse has designed and named origami butterflies to honor their pioneering work. While some are still active, others have sadly passed from our embrace—but not from our hearts. This book is lovingly dedicated as a memorial to the contributions of the late: Akira Yoshizawa, Lillian Oppenheimer, Alice Gray, Michael Shall, Eric Joisel, Emiko Kruckner, Killian Mansfield, Florence Temko, Joyce Rockmore, and V'Ann Cornelius.

The Mudarri Luna Moth and a Guy Kawasaki Swallowtail.

Tony Cheng
(page 38)

Jane Winchell
(page 40)

Alice Gray
(page 34)

Makoto Yamaguchi
(page 48)

Kyoko Kondo
(page 62)

Lillian Oppenheimer
(page 76)

Vanessa Gould
(page 52)

Sok Song
(page 72)

Jan Polish
(page 44)

Killian Mansfield
(page 66)

Eric Joisel
(page 68)

Robert Lang
(page 54)

Emiko Kruckner
(page 58)

Acknowledgments

We thank Tuttle Publishing for the opportunity to revisit our origami butterfly designs with both diagrams and video instructions to make these projects more accessible and enjoyable. We are grateful to our editor, Jon Steever, for his expert guidance and careful editing, and to the rest of the talented Tuttle team. We gratefully acknowledge the graphics design work of Greg Mudarri, who helped us with our first book of origami butterfly designs at Origamido Studio, and we thank him for his past contributions and continued friendship. Finally, these designs could not have been developed without the inspirational works of Akira Yoshizawa, who also influenced Russell Cashdollar. Their prior origami butterfly designs provided both seed and fertilizer for this Field of Discovery!

LEFT and RIGHT The tessellated fabric background is "Dodecagon Whirl Spools," folded silk, from *Shadowfolds* by Chris K. Palmer.

Contents

Before being spent, a piece of paper currency rests briefly in the form of an origami butterfly.

Guy Kawasaki (page 78)

The Origamido Butterfly (page 82)

The Question Mark (page 87)

Diana Wolf (page 90)

V'Ann Cornelius (page 92)

Doris Asano (page 88)

June Sakamoto (page 94)

Anne LaVin (page 98)

The Boston Butterfly (page 86)

The Mudarri Luna Moth (page 106)

Russell Cashdollar (page 103)

Kyoto (page 100)

Le Papillon de Nuit (page 109)

The Metamorphosis of an Origami Artist

by Richard Alexander, Origamido Studio Cofounder

Decorative paper folding has been around for at least a few hundred years in Japan, but this early repertoire seems to include only a few dozen models. In 1937, Akira Yoshizawa embraced origami as his occupation. By 1952, a commission by Asahi Graf for a new set of zodiac origami brought him fame. The response encouraged him to continue to design new origami in his own style of expressive paper folding. Yoshizawa is now considered by many to be the father of expressive art origami.

Michael G. LaFosse grew up in Fitchburg, Massachusetts. Even as a young child he was particularly good at making things of paper, and he worked his way through the craft and origami books at the local library. He was a teenager when he saw color photos of works by origami master Akira Yoshizawa in a 1970 article in *Reader's Digest*. This was the first time he realized it was possible to design your own origami. It was also the first origami he considered as expressive art, and he read that article over and over again. The powerful photos alone gave him the aspiration to become an origami artist! He realized that Yoshizawa's paper was much different than any he had seen—much heavier than any he had folded. Yoshizawa's paper allowed softer folds and expressive, curved lines.

Fortunately for him, Fitchburg was a paper-making town, so Michael was able to learn about paper-making processes and materials from his friends' parents who worked in the mills. Eventually he found a way to make whatever type of paper he needed for his folded art, and he soon learned to locate quality materials in the Boston area.

The origami books Michael had borrowed had mentioned Lillian Oppenheimer and her Origami Center of America in New York City. In 1977, Michael found himself in New York, and he paid an initial visit to Lillian. A short time later, he returned with his origami creations, and showed her his realistic bat, cattleya orchid, horseshoe crab, and several lifelike birds. Lillian invited several friends to see his works and to fold with Michael. He spent a week there, sleeping on Lillian's

couch, and met Michael Shall, who taught him how to fold Akira Yoshizawa's butterfly (from a waterbomb base). During this visit he also met Alice Gray, who worked in the entomology section at the American Museum of Natural History. She admired his complex praying mantis, and she invited him to see the insects at the museum. As they rode the subway uptown to the museum, Michael folded his first origami butterfly from a pink, 8½" x 11" piece of scrap paper. Alice admired it, but lamented it was not from a square. The bus trip back home to Fitchburg gave him hours for exploration, and he settled on three variations of the Butterfly for Alice Gray, each folded from a square.

At the time, Michael's complex models were dismissed by some in New York as "paper sculpture," and "not really origami" the way they saw it, so he did not return to New York for many years. Even so, he was still actively creating and folding origami art during that period. Most of his signature works were developed in that time. He even published and sold drawings for his origami F-14 Tomcat Fighter Jet (one of 28 original paper airplane designs that now appear in the hardcover book and DVD set, *Planes for Brains*, (Tuttle Publishing).

We met in 1988, when Michael was working as a chef, and folding in the wee hours of the morning after the restaurant had closed. His apartment had piles of crumpled paper, and I was overwhelmed by the beauty and complexity of his origami masterworks the first time I saw them. I found his work so spectacular, I offered to help him exhibit it, and soon we were mounting and framing it, videotaping his folding sequences, and making special papers in the garage. We set up exhibits at craft fairs and museums. Buoyed by the public's response, Michael called Lillian in 1991, and the timing could not have been more perfect. She invited him to a master class by Akira Yoshizawa in Ossining, New York, which is where he finally met Yoshizawa (as well as Emiko Kruckner, Jonathan Baxter, and other advanced folders from all over the country).

A Butterfly for Emiko Kruckner visits Michael's origami Munich Orchids.

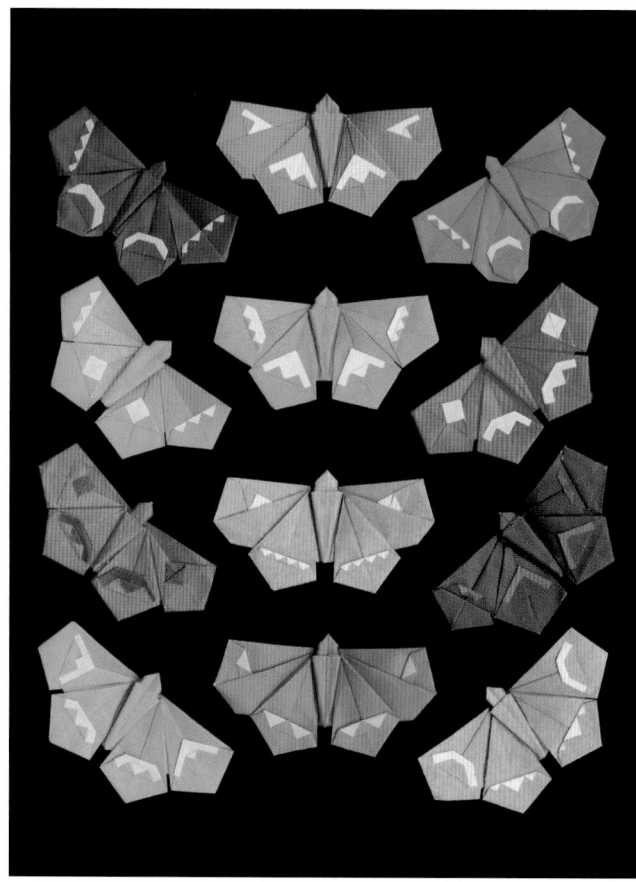 

Russell Cashdollar designed and folded this display of colorful origami butterflies, which inspired LaFosse to revisit and expand his own folded butterfly repertoire.

We met more serious origami artists at our first origami convention of the Friends of the Origami Center, held in 1992 at a public school in New York City. One of the more memorable and colorful displays was a collection of brightly patterned origami butterflies, designed and beautifully folded by Russell Cashdollar, a folder from the Washington, D.C. area.

Inspired by Russell's work, Michael recalled his Butterfly for Alice Gray that he'd designed and folded in 1978, and he began to revisit the potential for his butterfly base.

We recently called Russell to ask if he had a photo of those original butterflies from 1992 that we might add to this book. We began to reminisce with him about how his display had inspired Michael to revisit earlier works. Russell recalled that his butterflies had also prompted the noted origami creator and author, John Montroll, to explore a variety of models that displayed both sides of the paper. John published a remarka-

ble collection of such designs in his book, *Origami Inside-Out* (Antroll, 1993). After some extensive searching, Russell not only found his original models, he took a look at Michael's butterfly designs and went back to explore more variations of his own! He had originally started with a Yoshizawa butterfly design, and more recently has developed several new designs from frog and lily bases.

Lasell College invited Michael to set up a two-floor show of original origami art at their Yamawaki Art & Cultural Center in Newton, Massachusetts in 1994. The show included several butterflies folded from his handmade papers. We also released a self-published video folding tutorial, *Origami Butterflies & Moths* that provided close-up shots of Michael masterfully working the details—shaping, curling, and tweaking the models. He became a popular origami instructor at schools, libraries, and quite frequently at The Butterfly Place in Westford, Massachusetts, an amazing attraction developed and run by entomologist, George Leslie, and his family.

We also constructed large versions of Michael's origami butterflies for retail store window displays at Saks Fifth Avenue in New York City in 1993, and more recently for Hermes of Paris on Madison Avenue. In 1996, we opened the Origamido Studio, where we taught classes, made handmade paper, and framed art (including dozens of butterflies suitable for weddings, anniversaries, or birthdays). Even the scraps of our handmade papers became origami butterfly earrings and pins that we and our students enjoyed folding.

It's amazing to think that just a few photos of Yoshizawa's remarkable works from *Reader's Digest* in 1970 were enough to trigger an artistic metamorphosis! Michael's origami butterfly design system has evolved a great deal since he folded his first original model for Alice Gray in 1978. Decades later, this book distills Michael's lifetime of inventive, elegant, and pleasing origami butterfly designs. Their overall shape and presence, balance, and the interrelationship of line, form, and color must all be just right before Michael considers a design complete. He often thinks of the impact Yoshizawa's art had upon him, and wonders what young minds must be thinking when their eyes catch their first glimpse of a beautiful origami butterfly.

The Butterfly Project—at the Holocaust Museum, Houston

Several million people were imprisoned and put to death in the Nazi concentration camps. Only a few survivors were left to be liberated at the end of World War II, and it is important that their stories about the dangers of intolerance resonate with the next generation. There is now a special memorial in Texas at the Morgan Family Center's Holocaust Museum in Houston. Paper butterflies sent to the memorial represent the souls of 1,500,000 innocent children who perished in the Holocaust. For information about this memorial, visit *hmh.org*.

More than two thousand butterflies to be added to the hundreds of thousands already collected by the Holocaust Museum for the Butterfly Project. The museum's goal is to collect 1.5 million handmade butterflies to commemorate the children who perished in the Holocaust.

A collection of paper butterflies created for the Holocaust Museum's Butterfly Project by a tenth grade English class at Henrico High School in Henrico, VA.

The Exciting World of Origami Butterflies

by Richard Alexander, Origamido Studio Cofounder

This book contains print and video instructions for folding Michael G. LaFosse's favorite origami butterfly designs. We chose a new selection of models to illustrate his origami butterfly design system, a series of decisions and techniques that will allow you to discover an unlimited variety of butterfly "species" by mixing and matching folding maneuvers. Not only do the printed diagrams show how to fold them, the companion video DVDs show Michael explaining the steps as he folds. He also demonstrates wet-folding techniques (for creating lasting works of art from fine papers).

The Origamido Butterfly (page 82), folded from iridescent marbled paper.

A Butterfly for Alice Gray
(page 34)

A Butterfly for Emiko Kruckner
(page 58)

Poetry for the Fingers

Art in any form helps us cope with daily life. Michael's origami butterfly designs are "poems for the fingers," the folding of which is a particularly satisfying blend of relaxation and stimulation. There is a beautiful progression of musculoskeletal movements that advance naturally, as when keying a lyrical passage on a flute. You might feel the same way when you recite a favorite poem, stanza by stanza, or when you control phrasing and breathing to sing a song. If some of today's complex origami models are similar to epic novels, then these origami butterflies are short, sweet, love sonnets. To help you relax and enjoy learning these folds, we have included a few *haiku* thoughts for you to ponder along the journey.

when you love to sing
sad lyrics are forgotten
happy words burst forth!

Wet-folding allows the artist to sculpt graceful curves on this Mudarri Luna Moth (page 106).

A Serendipitous Journey

when was the last time
you jumped over a puddle
then over a tree?

The butterfly's metamorphosis symbolizes change, and the transformation of a single square piece of paper into a beautiful origami butterfly can be as unexpected and wonderful as a real butterfly's progress as it emerges from a cocoon.

Prepare for a delightful journey full of surprises! Discover the satisfying shapes and powerful personas of the butterflies you create. We recall the events that transpired or the places we were when we first folded each special origami butterfly, and often name them after that location or occasion. Let each butterfly remind you of happy times and gatherings. Spread the pleasure of folding and the joy of serendipity by sharing them with your friends. Hold them dearly in your hearts as we have!

Special Butterfly Names

special folding friends
become part of the table
and never leave us

From the beginning, Michael has named his favorite origami butterfly designs for the folding pioneers who spread the joy of origami through their creating, traveling, and teaching. Sometimes when he is exploring new combinations, proportions, and details, and he discovers something beautiful and unique, it can spontaneously remind him of a special origami ambassador, and then he names the piece for them. While it is difficult for him to explain, he does not set out to design a butterfly for a specific person, but rather, names a butterfly design only when it feels right.

The Question Mark
(page 87)

A Butterfly for Eric Joisel (page 68)

A Butterfly for Kyoko Kondo (page 62)

Origami Butterflies Have So Many Uses!

Butterflies are pollinators, and so origami butterflies have become a symbol, not only of change, but of communication, sharing, and the spread of knowledge. Fold butterflies with children to help them make their own personalized decorations for jackets, book bags, and backpacks. They are easily interchangeable when fastened with magnetic clips or Velcro dots. Use them for your own personal enjoyment, as earrings, pins, barrettes, and other origami jewelry.

We love to frame origami butterflies in shadowboxes for the wall. Use them to celebrate an important day—perhaps a wedding or anniversary. The First Wedding Anniversary is also known as The Paper Anniversary! When displayed in pairs, these butterflies often symbolize a special, joyful relationship.

When framed in small groups, we have used them to represent families, perhaps to welcome a child. They also make wonderful house-warming gifts. We often include mounted sequences (or step-folds) to symbolize metamorphosis, showing the steps from an open square to the finished butterfly. For the natural history lovers, Riker-box (compartmentalized display case) mounted, "vegetarian" butterfly collections of your favorite "fantasy species" could be just the right gift. Our more dramatic artistic presentations sometimes feature swarms of similar colors or styles, often on a handmade paper background representing grass, blossoms, or leaves.

Express your creativity with origami butterfly jewelry.

Wearable origami butterfly art is sure to garner compliments.

Paper butterflies make cheerful greeting cards, either as cover decorations (especially fitting for Mother's Day, graduations, St. Valentine's Day, get well, or friendship cards).

You can also fasten the butterfly inside the center of the card, and it will act as a pop-up element, flexing its wings when the card is opened.

There are dozens of appropriate social and office uses for origami butterflies as well. Use them to spice up banquet place cards, name tags, or ID badges. Instead of purchasing package bows or gift tags, fold a friendly origami butterfly.

When you receive a nicely wrapped gift, save some of the paper. Butterflies folded from squares cut from that wrap can become a thoughtful "thank you" that harkens back to the original present.

A beautiful butterfly provides the perfect finishing touch to gift wrapping.

An origami butterfly on a card lends a personal element that store bought cards just can't provide.

We all waste too much. Some discarded materials are quite beautiful, and suitable for reuse as origami butterflies. Convert pretty trash to treasure by folding up scraps of fine papers that are too small for other uses.

If you enjoy scrapbooking, fold butterflies for special remembrances from mementos of a joyful event. Save a special wrapper, brochure, or ticket stub from a memorable outing and incorporate it into your organized journal of an active life. Many folders also use scrapbooks for future folding reference, by mounting their favorite origami butterfly step-folds in the proper sequence. (Try using one or two-inch squares.) If the origami object becomes fully three dimensional in the final stages, simply substitute snapshots for the folded paper when documenting those closing steps.

Family gatherings and celebrations are perfect occasions to use color-coordinated origami butterfly decorations!

Accessorize your gifts of floral bouquets and house plants with a butterfly to add that special personal touch.

Origami butterflies make unique interior decorations and can be simply pinned to curtains or draperies. When guests are coming, use them instead of chocolates as a calorie-sparing pil-

low adornments in the guest room. Set the table with origami butterflies affixed to candlesticks (away from flames, of course), napkin rings, or to personalize each guest's wineglass.

Origami butterflies love to travel, especially through the mail. As "puzzle" notes, write your note on the square first, and then fold it and send it in an envelope with its wings closed!

Last year, during the holidays, we enjoyed a cheerful tree, stringing origami butterflies with bright ribbon and a bead to become festive, hanging ornaments.

The United States and many nations have interesting paper currency, so fold some cash into butterflies to use as tips or gifts (see page 23 for more).

The butterfly in this card symbolically spreads its wings when opened.

Congratulations!

Graduate

Ascend Emerge

camps love to discover new crafting activities, and it is a good fit to incorporate recycling activities with origami crafts to cut down on expenses for materials.

Some people love to fold paper for relaxation, and they enjoy its meditative, zen-like aspects. Folding origami butterflies may also have a place in physical therapy for patients who need to keep their hands active, but become bored when folding the same design. Creating different origami butterflies challenges the mind and keeps it active. A local therapist found that origami provided a unique way for her patients to let go of sad or painful issues by folding related documents. Similarly, it can be a creative way to keep happy notes or love letters!

Some people do not realize that designing elegant origami requires time, talent, and money. Modern origami designs are the intellectual property of the artist, and commercial uses require agreements with the artist for consent to terms of use, royalties, and other conditions. Our company, Origamido, Inc., licenses our own origami designs for commercial uses (just as Yoshizawa did with his art many years ago. He

An Alexander Aztec Swallowtail visits a bouquet for mom.

If your community has a citizens' center, or seniors' center, introduce origami butterfly folding as a creative pastime. Activity coordinators for after-school programs and summer

Richly patterned and exceptionally durable, paper currency is an attractive choice for folding origami butterflies.

never sold any of his 50,000 origami, thanks to licensing photos of his work to advertisers.)Whether designed for the conventional, printed page, or for web-based advertising, origami garners attention. Business logos for letterhead, envelopes, calling cards, props for TV commercials, and even tangible advertising can be specifically designed and licensed by Origamido, Inc.

Clients have used some of our butterfly designs to grace their retail store windows, signs, posters, or billboards. You do not need our permission to use these designs for your own non-commercial use, but please respect our rights and be sure to request permission for any commercial use. Contact *info@origamido.com* to make the necessary arrangements.

A special, limited edition commission for Lalique, on the release of their glass pattern, *Vibrations*.

BELOW This Origamido butterfly measured eleven feet from tip to tip, and was the first piece of art commissioned by the Peabody Essex Museum in Salem, Massachusetts for their new atrium. We suspended it near the entrance to their year-long exhibit of origami art, "Origami Now!"(June, 2007 to June, 2008). The sculpture was folded by the authors from 100% cotton watercolor paper by the authors, and each wing was supported by aluminum rods. It required disassembly for transport!

Using Fine Quality Art Materials

When you want your butterflies to last for many generations without fading or becoming brittle, be sure to use only fine art-quality materials. Art papers are formed from stronger fibers and so they are more durable when wet-folding. These resiliant papers allow a more artistic shaping than do machine-made papers of highly processed wood pulp. High quality papers for fine art use cost more because they are made of more expensive raw materials (choice fibers and archival pigment colorants). The market for fine art materials is small, and so the machinery is smaller and less efficient. In fact, many fine art papers are still made by hand, so labor costs represent a larger fraction of the final price. Although many university arts programs have hand paper-making equipment, and although student labor is less expensive, fine art origami paper making is still a relatively new field. Few art students currently make thin, strong sheets suited to folding, and they are more likely to prepare pulp for cast paper sculptures, or to form thicker sheets from unusual plants, including unprocessed parts (seeds or twigs) that impede creasing.

Richly colored, densely patterned, often accented with gold, Yuzen papers make the most lovely of origami butterflies. The papers are durable and can be purchased from specialty paper suppliers. If you can't get to one in person, shop online where you can see images of the patterns being offered for sale.

Paper or plastic? Many art and craft supply shops offer foldable sheets in a dazzling array of new materials. Pearlescent plastic sheets come textured and smooth, and in a rainbow of colors.

100% cotton rag-content drafting papers are thin, strong, and translucent—perfect for folding butterflies that reveal the pattern of hidden folds and layers. The paper comes in pads and rolls, and is widely available. Look for tinted tracing papers, too.

The organic, lyrical, swirling, and feathered patterns of marbled papers seem to mimic nature and are displayed marvelously on the wings of an origami butterfly. If you cannot find the selection you desire, make it yourself! Marbling supplies and instructions are widely available. You will enjoy the surprise of your own, happy results!

Most stores that carry fine papers specialize in wedding invitations, but may also carry hand marbled and fancy printed sheets that could become beautiful origami butterflies. Countless shades of handmade paper from Asia and India are on the market today, but many of the commonly used dyes fade quickly. When you are selecting stock at fine papers stores, examine the exposed margins of display sheets for signs of fading, and ask the experts if they know the colorfastness ratings of the papers they stock. Look for the words "acid free" and "archival" on the labels. (Even with these designations, we have seen some of these papers fade.)

At Origamido Studio, we design and make our own custom papers for each piece of exhibition-quality folded art. We have found that fiber from specially grown plants, including abaca, hemp, cotton, flax, mitsumata, gampi, and kozo (also called paper mulberry) works best for our folded art. We sometimes cook and clean the fibers, and always beat and condition the pulp ourselves. That way, we can confidently control the other variables that affect the characteristics of the paper with reliable results. Our workshops for other origami artists show them how to make the perfect paper for their art.

The project photos for this book were all folded from Origamido duo papers. We applied a water soluble adhesive between two sheets of different colors, pressed, and then dried them again to make duo sheets. (We use methyl cellulose gel, a refined food additive that is also commonly sold as wallpaper paste.) Since butterfly wings have tiny scales, we often add

ground mica mineral when coloring the pulp slurry to lend a beautiful sheen to the finished paper's surface.

If this sounds like too much work, take heart. White or neutral Japanese *washi* (a term that refers to any high quality paper made in Japan, but often made from mulberry pulp) is available at art store chains and from Internet suppliers. It is easy to customize *washi* to make it any shade you want using artist-quality acrylic paints. Some of the butterflies in our photographs also sport acrylic washes of iridescent paint applied to our own Origamido papers. These paints are formulated for airbrush application, but also work well when applied by brush, and are available in most art supply stores. For more information, we discuss making, selecting, and preparing fine papers for lasting art in our book, *Japanese Paper Crafting*. Our other art titles, *Advanced Origami*, and *Origami Art* (all from Tuttle Publishing) may also be of interest to the aspiring origami artist.

ABOVE Luscious, archival, and destined to become butterflies, these Origamido papers are handmade by Michael LaFosse and Richard Alexander.

BELOW LEFT Why not make your own, custom handmade papers? Paper making supplies and kits are easy to find. Small, letter paper sized sheets are easy to make and don't require a major setup in your home. Your custom-made papers will make very special keepsakes of your butterflies.

RIGHT A display rack of handmade Origamido paper at Origamido Studio.

Getting Started

All you need is a rectangle. Michael folded his first original origami butterfly for Alice Gray in 1978 from a discarded piece of pink office paper on the subway. You can generate many suitable rectangles just by folding in the opposite edges of a square.

These butterfly designs show both sides of the sheet, and you will find many kinds of paper that make beautiful butterflies. So-called "regular" origami paper has color on only one side (it's white on the other). We folded with regular origami paper to demonstrate each project on the accompanying DVDs.

Squares

Found Rectangles

Common Office and Letter Size Papers

$ Dollar Bills

Origami paper now comes in a remarkable number of "Duo" color and print forms.

Play money and candy wrappers are transformed by origami.

Origami paper with two (non-white) colors is called "duo." You can fold great looking butterflies from any two-colored paper: regular or duo origami papers, paper-backed foils, two-color (duo) foils, duo prints, or print / solid duo papers. Enjoy practicing with scraps of gift wrap, colorful junk mail, or even packaging such as candy wrappers.

If you want your butterflies to last without fading, turning yellow, or becoming brittle, then be sure to use premium fiber papers marked "archival," or "acid free." Papers that have been pigmented with colorfast artist-quality materials last the longest.

Foil gift wrap makes a stunning display when folded into origami butterflies, and will serve well as a substitute for a package bow.

Origami Symbols Key

The origami diagrams used in this book are an efficient, internationally standardized system of lines and arrows, dots, dashes, and a few other symbols. Although simple, it is not immediately intuitive, so please invest a few moments to study the key, and refer back to it as needed. Become familiar with the symbols and what they mean. As you watch the DVDs, look at the corresponding diagrams in the book to reinforce your understanding. For efficiency, a diagram may contain more than one instruction, so check carefully for details you might have overlooked at first. If you are unsure of a step, glancing ahead to the next step often reveals the desired shape, and may provide other valuable clues. For your comfort, rotate the paper away from you as you fold it (even though the diagrams won't always show the object rotated), and then return it to the position shown in the diagram as you compare the shapes. Once you learn this elegant diagramming system, you'll be able to enjoy countless origami books.

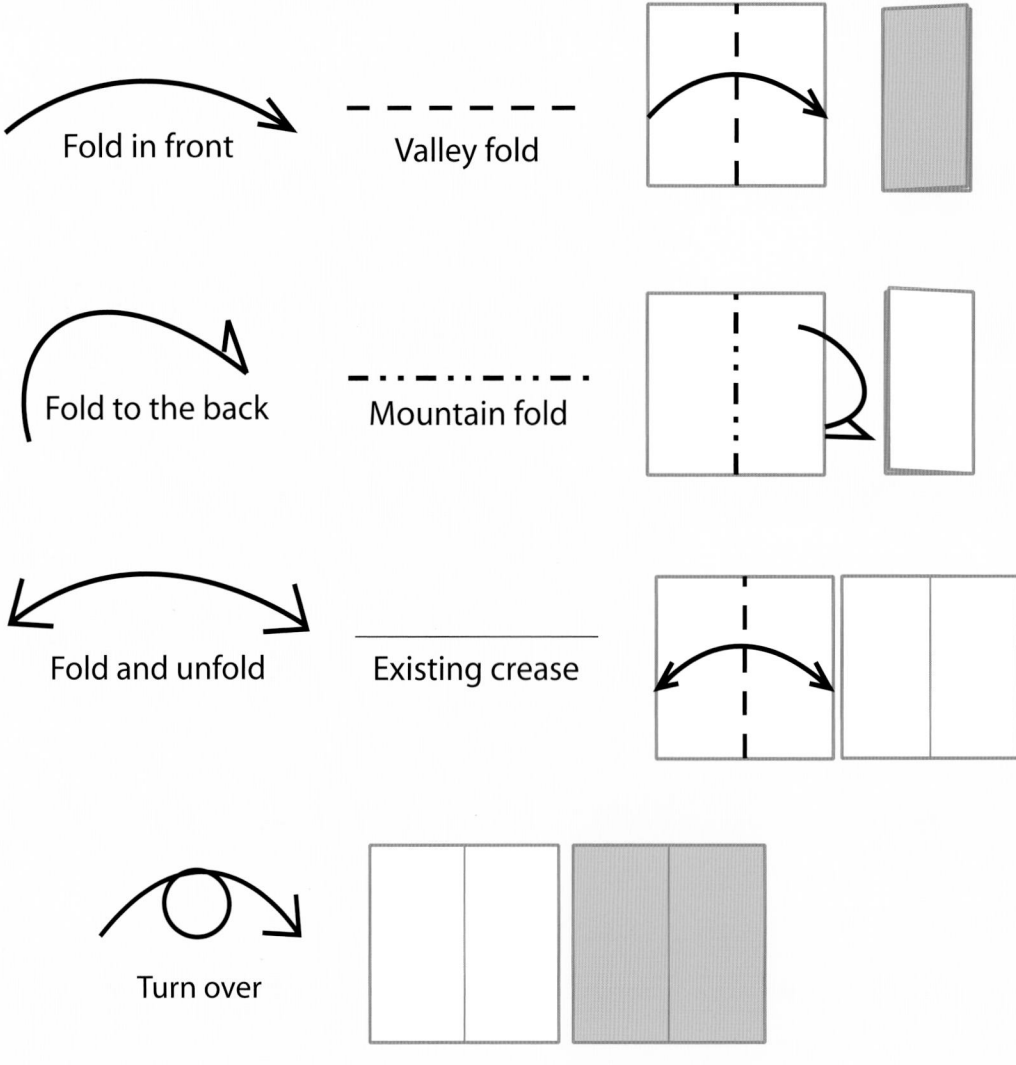

Fold in front

Valley fold

Fold to the back

Mountain fold

Fold and unfold

Existing crease

Turn over

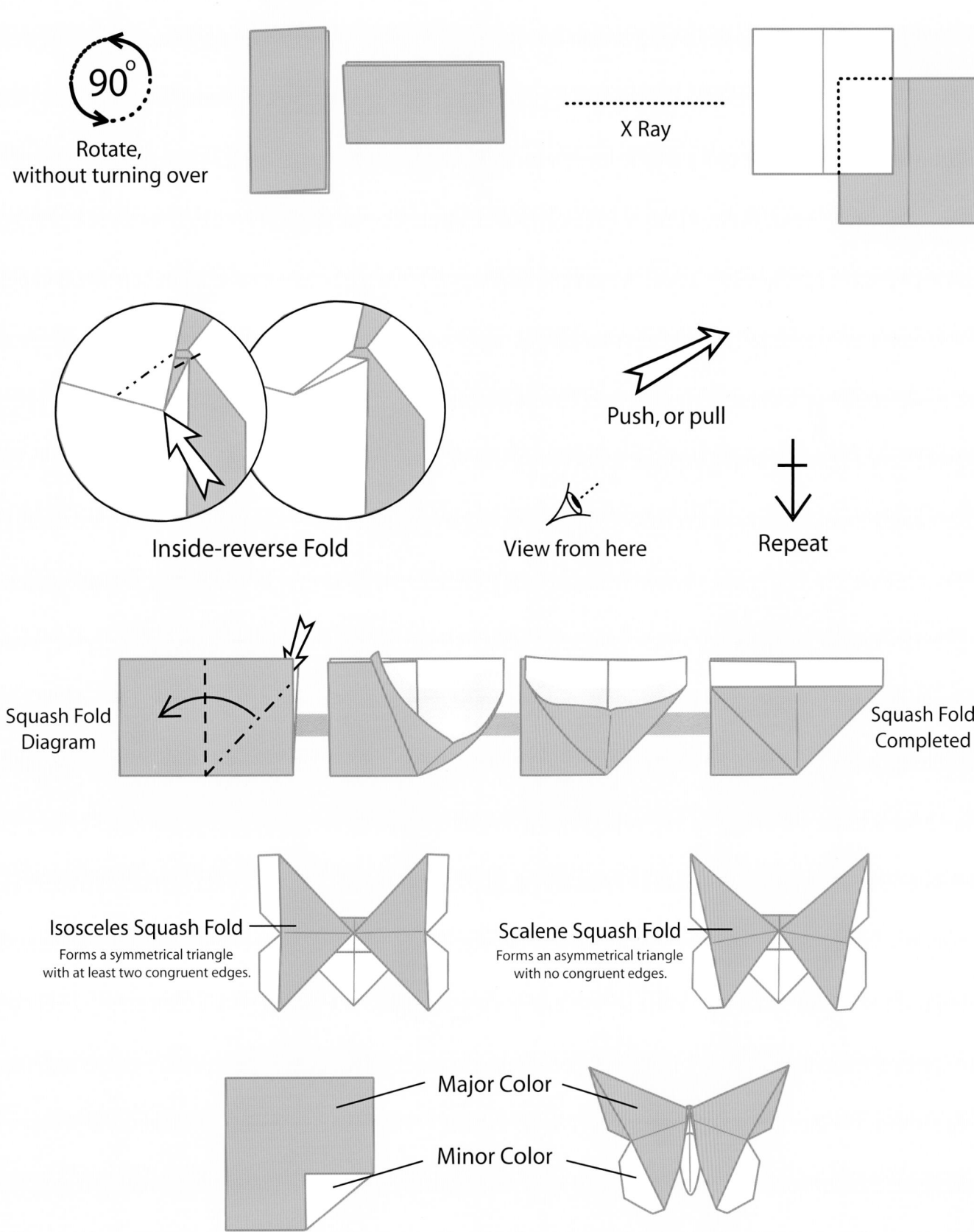

90°
Rotate,
without turning over

X Ray

Inside-reverse Fold

Push, or pull

View from here

Repeat

Squash Fold
Diagram

Squash Fold
Completed

Isosceles Squash Fold
Forms a symmetrical triangle
with at least two congruent edges.

Scalene Squash Fold
Forms an asymmetrical triangle
with no congruent edges.

Major Color

Minor Color

The Base Architecture

No matter how simple or complex any of the butterflies from our system may be, they each display many of the distinguishing features of their living counterparts: head, thorax, abdomen, forewings, and hindwings.

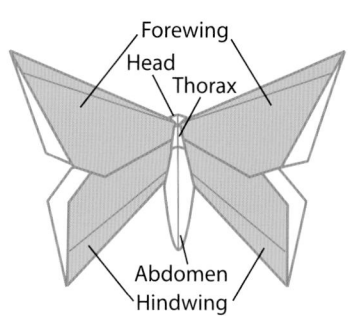

You will soon be defining all of these exciting features, but we need to begin with the foundation of the basic architecture that Michael developed in 1978 with his Butterfly for Alice Gray (page 34). Find a piece of letter paper and fold along with us as shown in the next few diagrams.

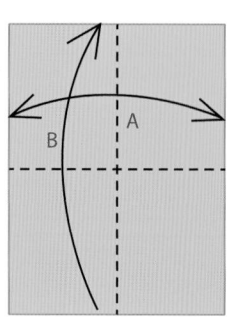

1. (A) Valley-fold in half, long edge to long edge. Unfold. (B) Valley-fold short edge to short edge.

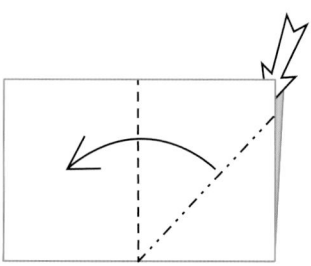

2. Squash-fold the right half. Look ahead at steps 3–5 to understand the process.

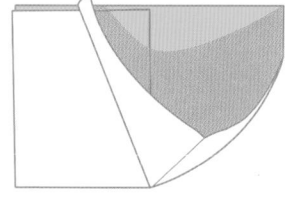

3. The squash fold in progress.

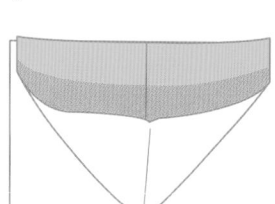

4. The squash fold almost complete. Press flat.

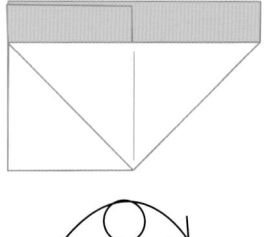

5. Your paper should look like this. Turn over, left to right.

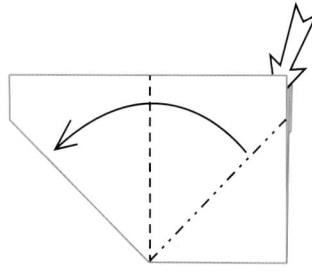

6. Squash-fold the right half.

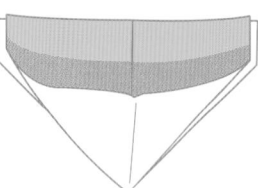

7. The squash fold in progress. Press flat.

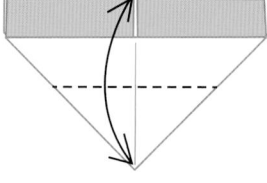

8. Valley-fold the bottom corner to the top of the split. Unfold.

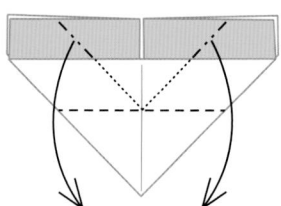

9. Squash-folding the right and left halves to form the wings.

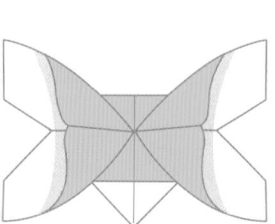

10. The squash fold in progress. Press flat.

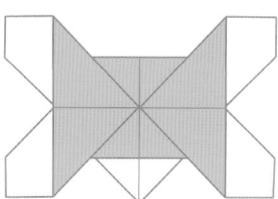

11. The "LaFosse Butterfly Base."

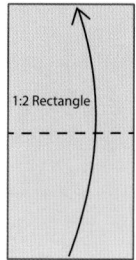

1. Fold in half, bottom to top.

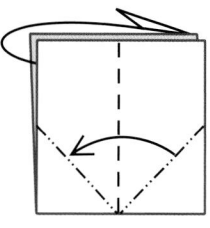

2. Squash-fold, and then flip and repeat on the reverse.

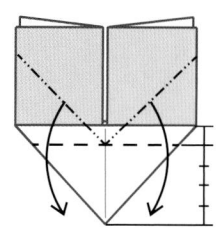

3. Valley-fold the bottom corner to the top of the split. Unfold. Squash-fold the left and right halves to form the wings.

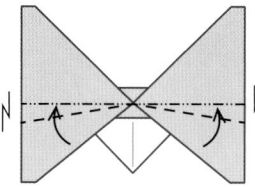

4. Move the top layers of each hindwing upward. Mountain-fold the existing horizontal crease and add a valley fold below, forming a crimp in the middle of each wing.

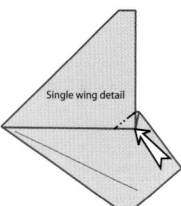

5. Inside-reverse-fold the corners of each wing.

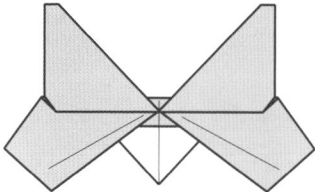

6. The "Dollar Bill Butterfly Base." Complete the butterfly by following finishing steps for other projects described in the book.

RIGHT Some rectangles, such as those used for most paper money, will produce bases with top-layers that extend beyond the normal wing margins of the base, and will usually provide no margin of paper for the head and thorax. However, you can make a head/thorax margin out of the upper 5th of the body paper, as shown in step 3, and you will need to form a crimp, as shown in steps 4 and 5, to differentiate the forewings and hindwings.

Customizing the Base for Variety

When preparing a base, place the first fold, or "horizon" crease, along the center by matching the lower edge to the upper edge (just fold the sheet in half). This is the butterfly's "waistline," separating forewings from hindwings. (A short portion will become the head and abdomen). Sharp creases are essential, so burnish every crease with the back of your thumbnail. (Or use a folding tool, a "bone folder," or even the bowl of a spoon. Do not use anything that can bruise or mar the paper's surface.) Placing the horizon crease above the center of the square will create smaller forewings and larger hindwings; placing it below will do the reverse. Open the paper. Keep the horizon crease horizontal.

There are many ways to form margins that result in a rectangle of suitable proportion. When measuring distances along the edge of the square, we like to make a short pinch as a reference mark at the edge (do not make a full length crease). Beginners may prefer to pinch a reference point along the other edge too, especially when folding a narrow margin flap accurately.

OPPOSITE LEFT AND RIGHT These early steps determine many possible outcomes. The photos show the initial set-up decisions (at left), and the resulting bases (at right) for some favorite butterfly models.

BELOW These diagrams show how to fold different proportions that contribute to the wide variety of origami butterfly bases from which to choose.

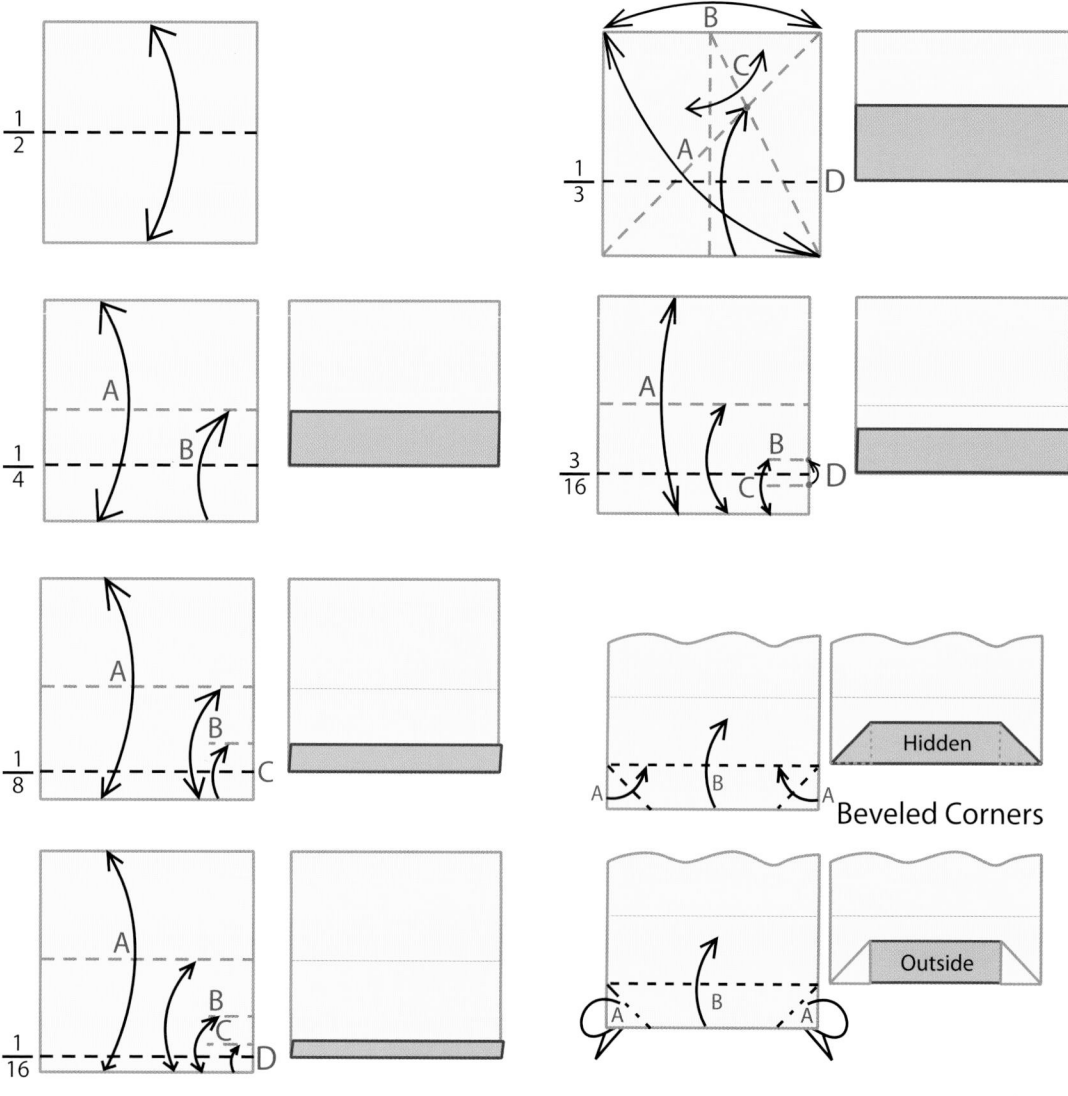

The photos to the left show some of the most common base variables.

LEFT In the top example you can see the effect of beveling the corners of the visible flap: triangular eyespots appear on the forewings.

BELOW LEFT Each setup will always provide you with two alternatives: fold in half to the front (for the result on the right) or fold in half to the back (for the result on the left). A different base results in each case.

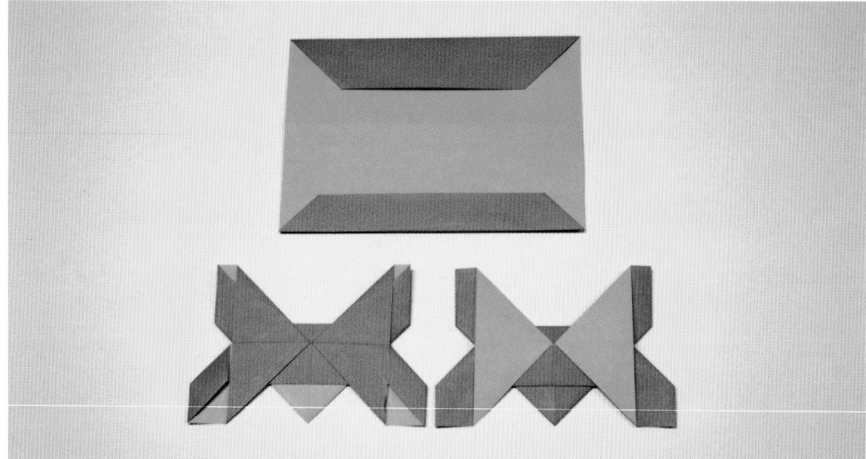

BOTTOM There are numerous combinations and possibilities regarding the orientation and size of margin flaps and corners. The margin flaps can be folded to the front, to the back, or with one on each side. The most versatile initial setup approximates the ratio of the Golden Rectangle, and when you fold over a pair of $\frac{3}{16}$ flaps, the resulting rectangle's ratio of length to width will be within 2% of the Golden proportion! We routinely do this by first pinching marks at the $\frac{1}{4}$, and at $\frac{1}{8}$ positions, and then by aligning one pinch on top of the other, and creasing all the way across the square (along the midpoint between the two reference pinch marks), you will have defined a flap measuring $\frac{3}{16}$ as wide as the square. Repeat with the opposite edge. Some designs require the corners of these margins to be folded—some to the outside, others tucked beneath.

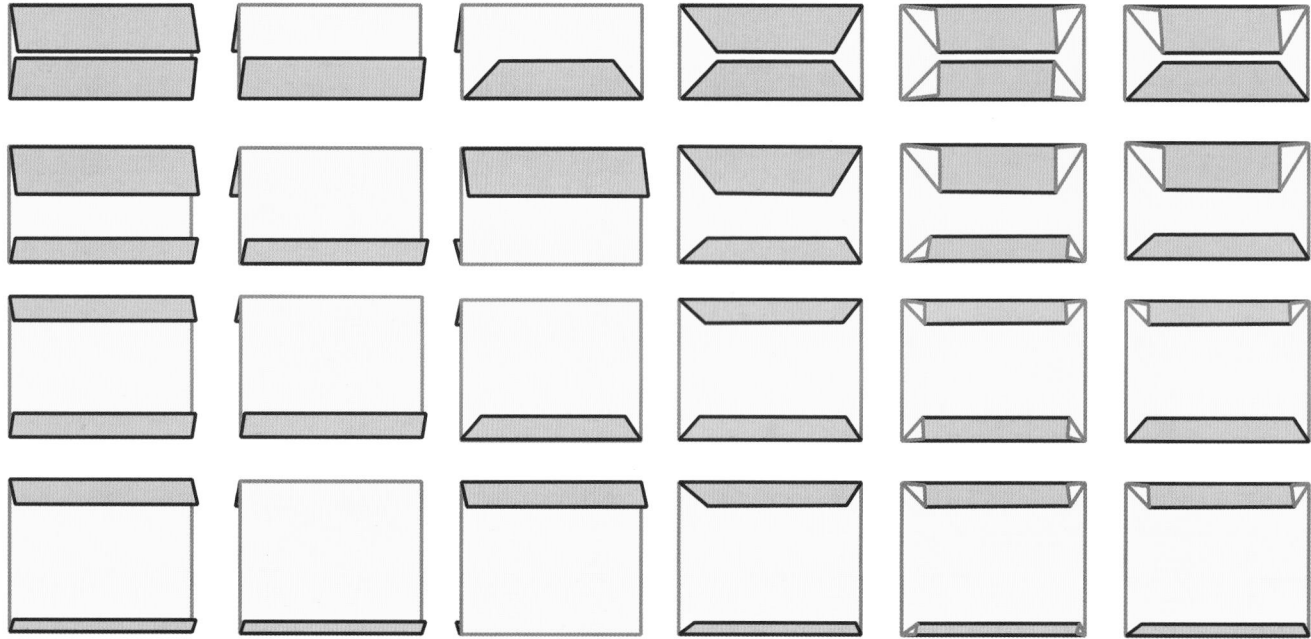

The Turning Point

After the margins and corners are set, the next fold (mountain or valley) determines the display side of the butterfly. When you fold the paper in half, the surface inside that fold will become the major display surface of the wings.

BELOW Note the different outcomes! Another consequence of this key decision is whether the flaps and corners become trapped or free. This will impact the finishing detail possibilities.

Permutations of this base (for the Butterfly for Alice Gray—page 34) can be generated from a variety of margin and corner choices. Three major categories of crease patterns define the resulting permutations. The "A" series all have rectangular margin flaps. The "B" series shows the possibilities when the corners of only one flap are beveled. For each folding plan, the front view (left) and back view (right), appear above their associated preliminary folds.

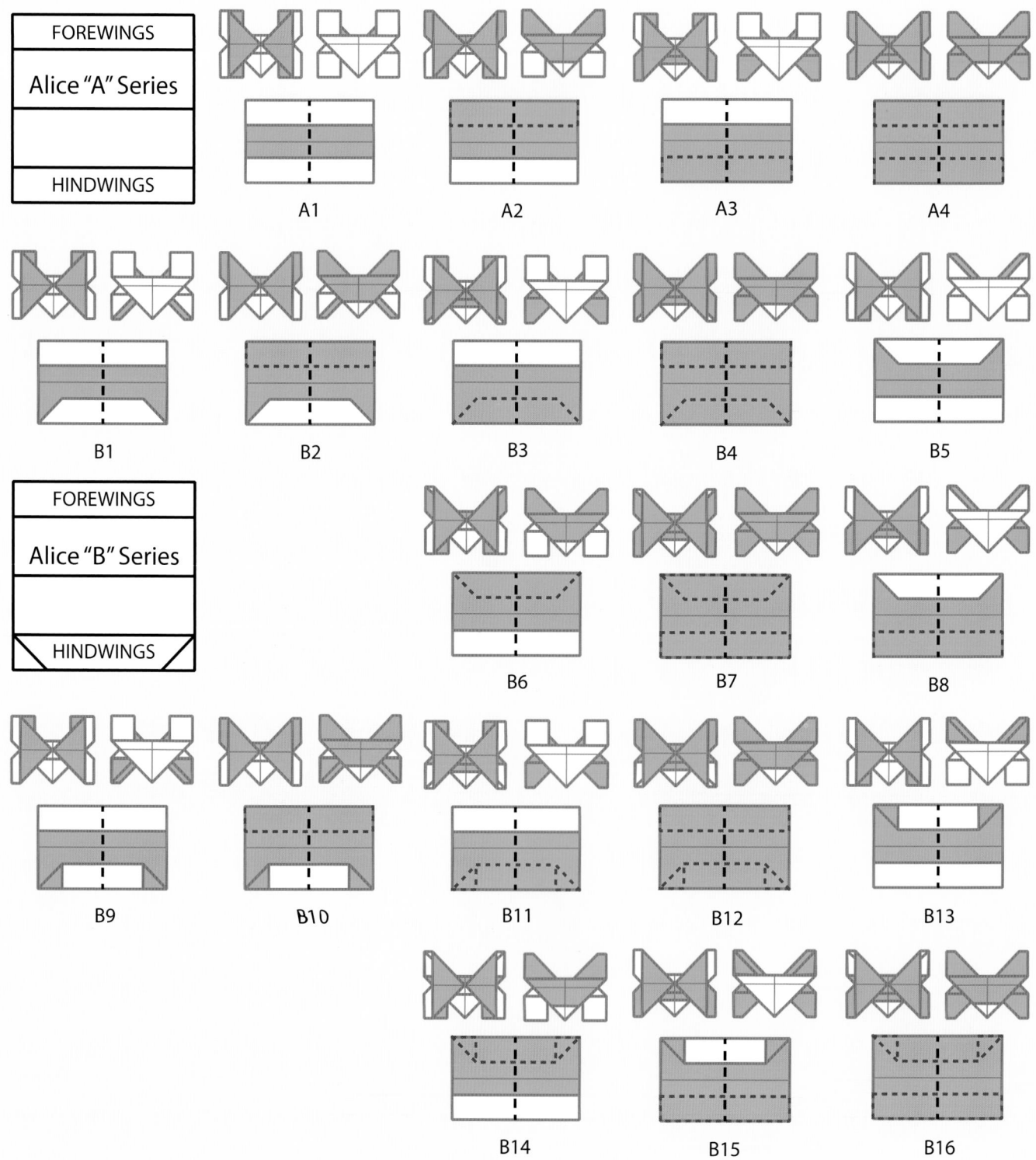

The "C" series shows the possible results after beveling the corners on both margin flaps. (Note that the margin proportions have not been changed.)

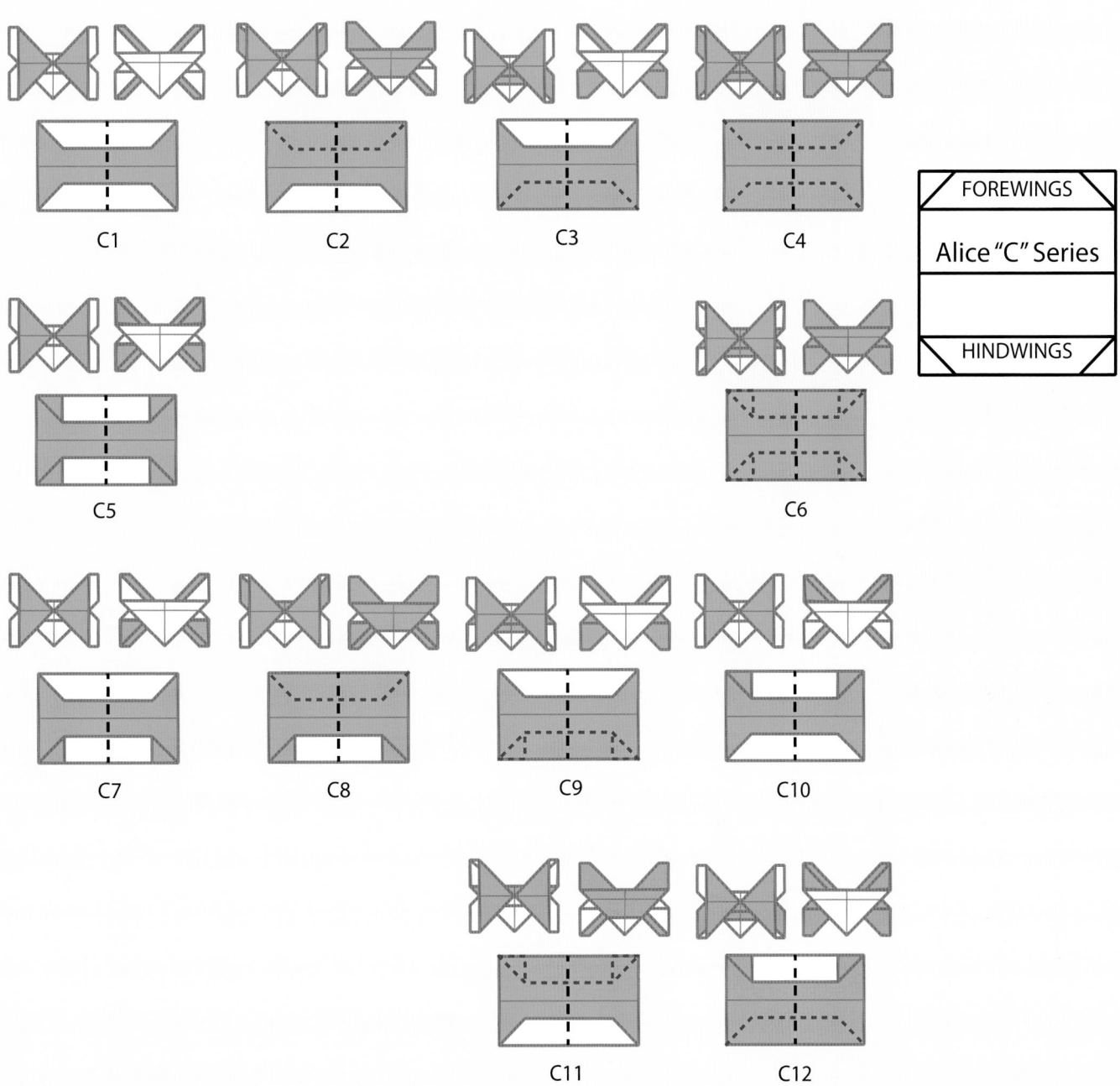

Wing Styles and Variations

Just as we have shown permutations of flaps, corners, and margins using the base for the Butterfly for Alice, this photo shows only a small fraction of different possible wing treatments. Favorite wing styles include variations of full-wings, forewings, and hindwings.

BELOW: The sky's the limit when it comes to configuring butterfly wings!

Right angles are unusual in nature's creatures, so your butterfly will look less artificial after you soften any perpendicular lines. Finishing the outer edges of the wings with special, folded treatments often takes advantage of the excess paper temporarily stowed in the margins and corners during the initial setup. Pull this excess paper out to create color change spots, patterns, or prongs. Another popular treatment involves shaping the tip of the forewing corner, often with a fold-over, inside-reverse, or even a small rabbit-ear fold.

These designs feature several favorite treatments, including rows of contrasting color triangles ("Aztec," as seen in "The Cashdollar," page 103), pivoting fanfolds (see "The June," page 94), color-change frame surrounds (see "The Jan," page 44), swallowtails (see "The Guy Kawasaki Swallowtail," page 78), pronghorns (see "The Lang," page 54), as well as regular, and irregular polygonal spots. These are just a few, so rest assured as you embark on your journey that there are plenty more to discover. We tend to favor the finished look of folded edges, but a splendid row of triangular spots from simple fan-folding can also be quite striking. The following illustration shows just a few of the wing shaping options.

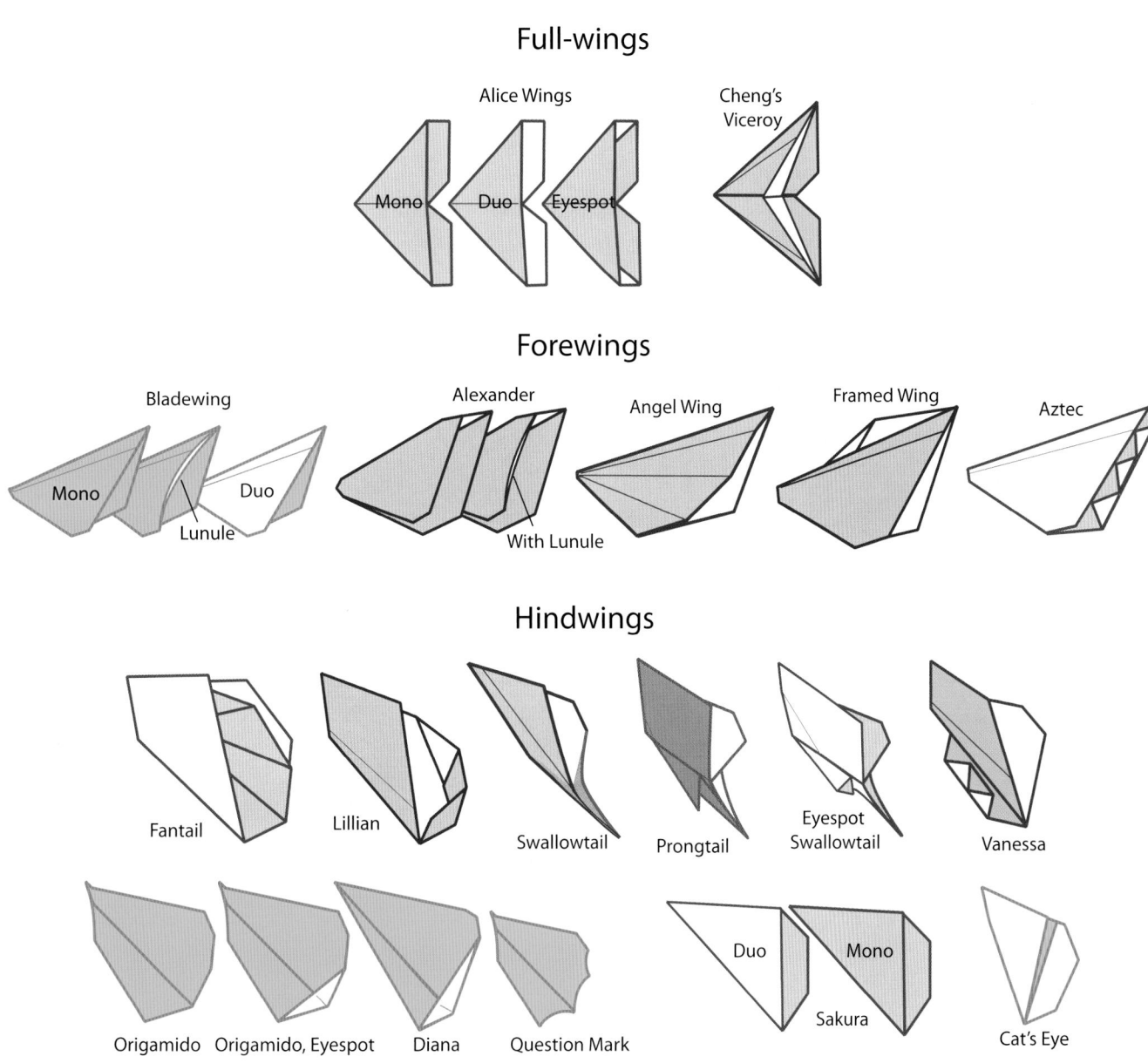

Full-wings

Alice Wings

Cheng's Viceroy

Mono   Duo   Eyespot

Forewings

Bladewing

Mono   Duo

Lunule

Alexander

With Lunule

Angel Wing

Framed Wing

Aztec

Hindwings

Fantail

Lillian

Swallowtail

Prongtail

Eyespot Swallowtail

Vanessa

Origamido   Origamido, Eyespot   Diana   Question Mark

Duo   Mono

Sakura

Cat's Eye

These Are a Few of My Favorite Wings

Lunule

A *lunule* is a simple, crescent-shaped reversal along the edge between the two layers that exposes the contrasting color when both layers of paper are the same color. This striking sliver formed by rolling the edge can be applied on either the forewing or hindwing.

Swallowtail

One of the most elegant shapes for the hindwing tips is a simple, mountain fold with an outward curl—a *swallowtail*. Wet folding will allow you to shape it easily. Moisten the paper slightly with a fine mist or damp cloth, and allow the moisture to penetrate before you shape the piece. Restrain the shaped paper in the desired position with a strip of cloth as it dries, to make the shape permanent. Too much moisture may abrade the surface or cause it to look fuzzy. (If you are uncomfortable with wet-folding, then fold foil swallowtails. They will hold their shape without any need for water!)

Aztec

Simple fan-folding along a diagonal produces rows of regular, alternating, triangular spots—the *Aztec* wing treatment. The Aztecs and others throughout the history of art produced designs featuring this popular motif. (The Z sound in the word "Aztec" helps our young students remember the zig-zagged, triangular pattern).

Butterfly Discovery Challenge

Michael LaFosse has developed and folded over a thousand different origami butterfly designs, and we'll show you how to fold some of his favorites in this book and accompanying DVDs. The following photos show a mere twenty-five of his favorite forewing and hindwing combinations. As you master the designs in this book, return to this page to see if you can figure out how each was folded!

BELOW: Frame tail wing variations.

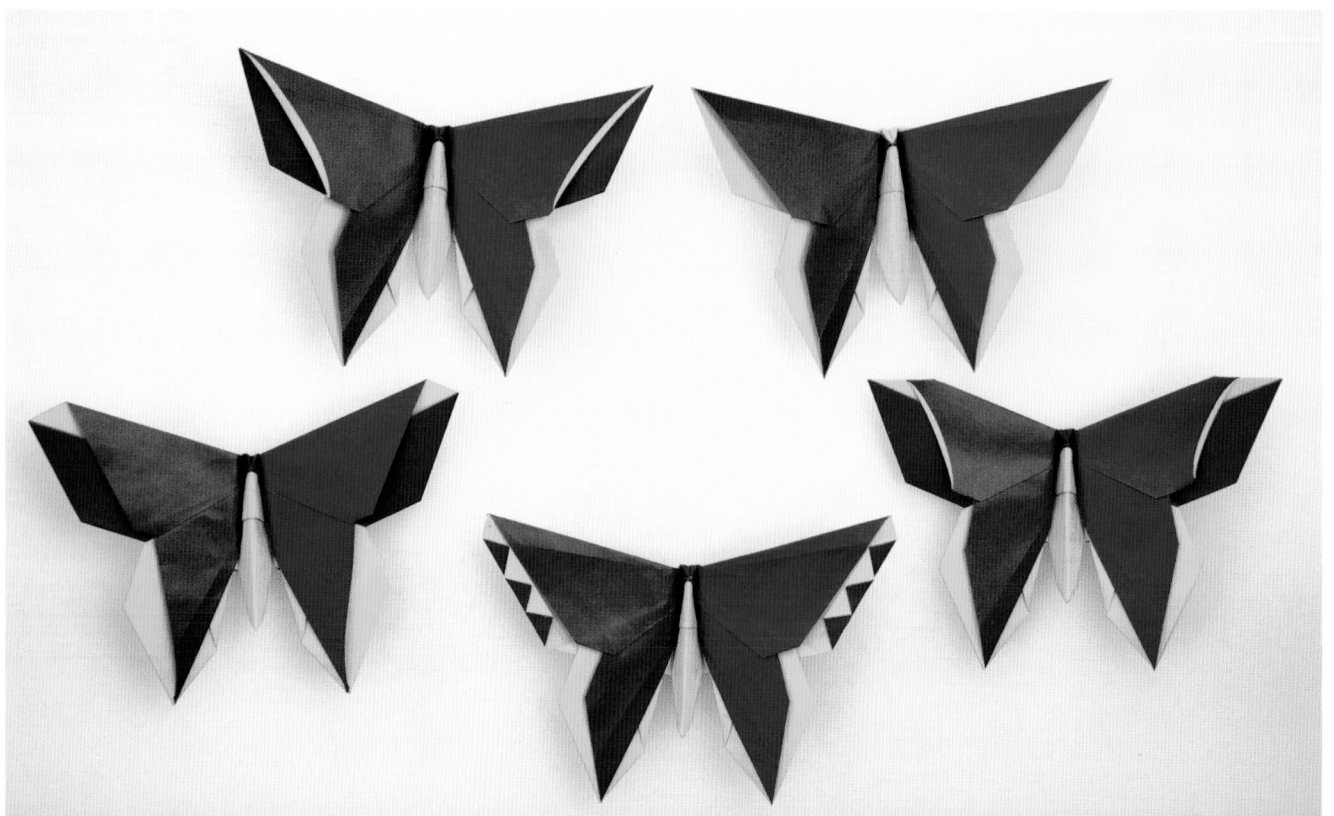

Prong Tail wing variations.

Sakura wing variations.

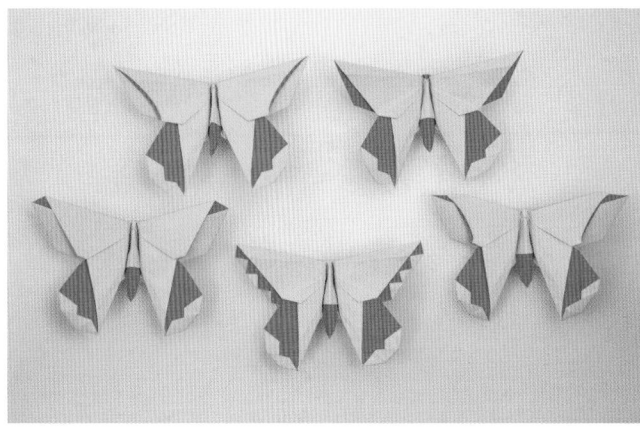

Lillian wing variations.

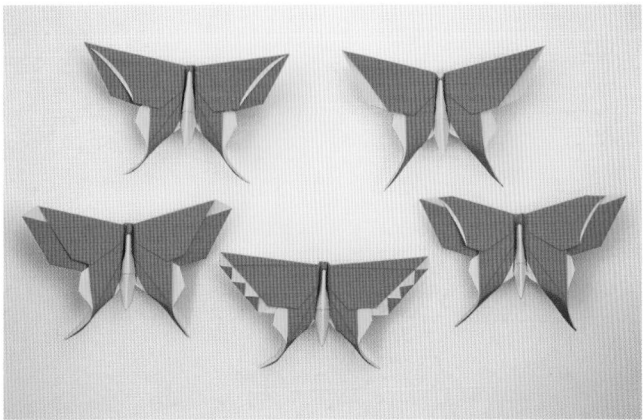

Swallowtail wing variations.

A Butterfly for Alice Gray

"The Alice"

This design is named for the late Alice Gray, entomological assistant, avid folder, teacher, and origami proponent. She was a crucial ally in bringing the offices of the national folding organization to the American Museum of Natural History in New York City.

This design was Michael's first original origami butterfly, and so "The Alice" is our matriarch of the family, having given life to the others that followed. She knows what makes them flap, and where to locate the best host plants for lunch. "The Alice" travels the world, introducing the joy of origami to the scientific types, while she also excites young children as they open their eyes to the natural wonders around them.

> *oh Lady of Bugs*
> *showing knowledge conquers fear*
> *hugging millipede!*

This design introduces the breadth of the potential of Michael's system. Explore the permutations and combinations possible from choosing different arrangements of margin flaps and corners, sometimes with beveled corners. Use a square (four to ten inches works best with most papers). A six-inch square produces a four-inch butterfly.

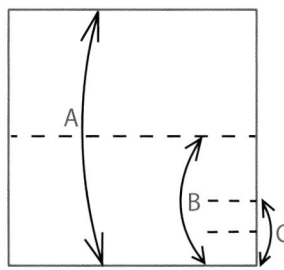

1. (A) Valley-fold in half, bottom edge to top edge. Unfold. (B) Align the bottom edge to the center crease and make a short pinch mark at the 1/4 point. Unfold. (C) Align the bottom edge to the first pinch mark and make another short pinch mark at the 1/8 point. Unfold.

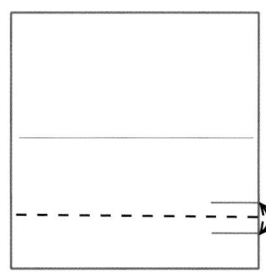

2. Lay the lower pinch mark on top of the upper pinch mark and valley-fold the flap halfway between the two pinch marks (the margin is now 3/16th of the square). Crease all along the width. Unfold.

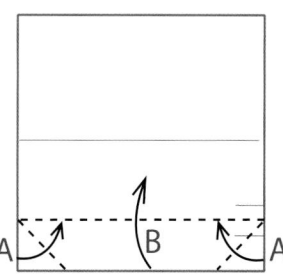

3. (A) Valley-fold the bottom left and right corners to the valley crease above. (B) Valley-fold the flap upward to lock the corners inside.

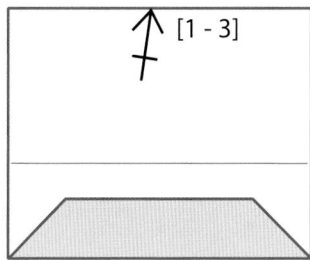

4. Repeat steps 1–3 with the opposite edge.

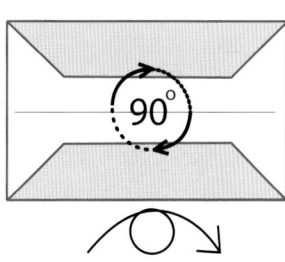

5. Rotate the paper 90 degrees clockwise. Turn the model over.

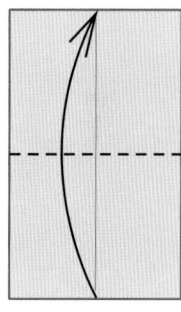

6. Valley-fold the bottom edge to the top.

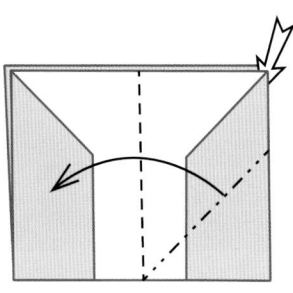

7. Squash-fold the right half. Look ahead to step 8 and 9 to see results.

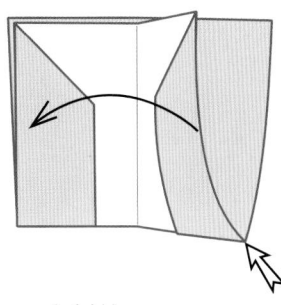

8. The squash-fold in progress.

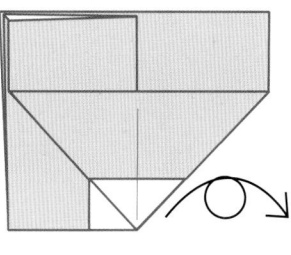

9. Your paper should look like this. Turn over, left to right.

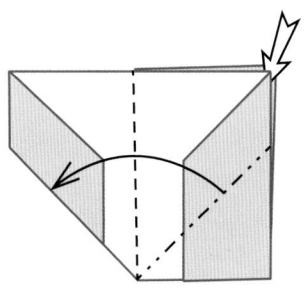

10. Squash-fold the right half.

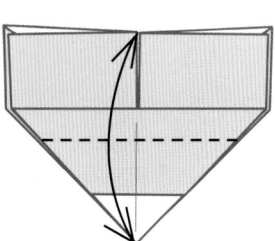

11. Valley-fold the bottom corner to the middle of the top edge. Unfold.

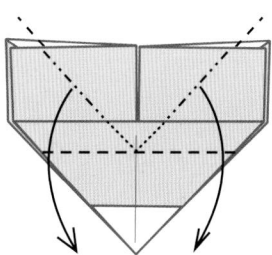

12. One at a time, squash-fold the right and left halves of the model to form the wings. Look ahead at step 13 for the shape.

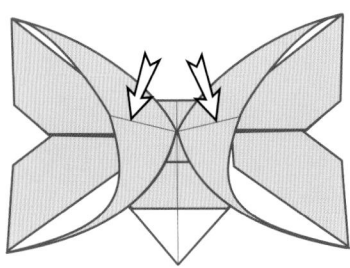

13. The squash-folds in progress.

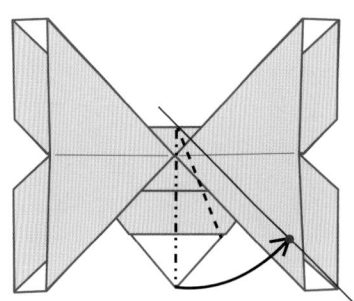

"Butterfly for Alice Base"

14. Your paper should look like this. This is the "Butterfly for Alice Base." Mountain-and valley-fold the abdomen over the right wing.

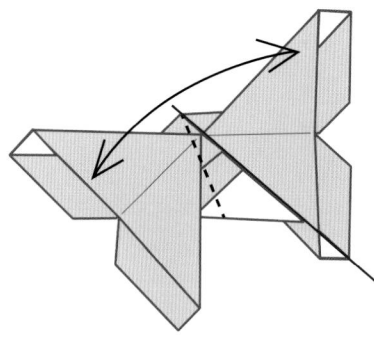

15. Valley-fold the left wing to match the right wing. Unfold.

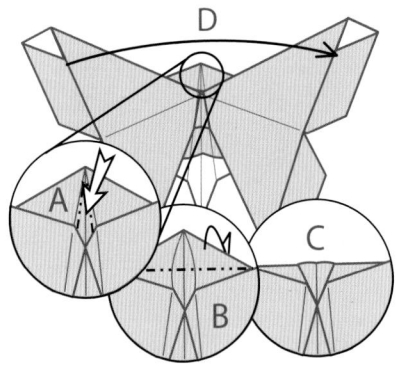

16. (A) Squash-fold the paper for the head. (B) Mountain-fold the corner behind. (C) Your paper should look like this. (D) Fold the wings together.

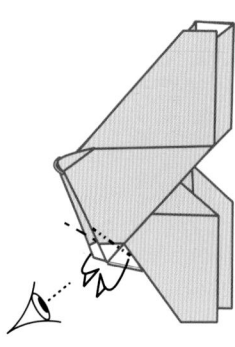

17. Mountain-fold the abdomen edges inside. See step 18 for the detail view.

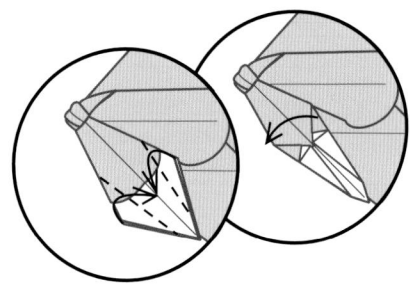

18. The view from the underside. Fold the lower edges of the abdomen inward. Close the abdomen.

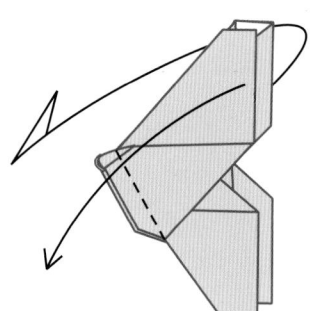

19. Valley-fold the wings down on each side.

A Butterfly for Alice Gray.

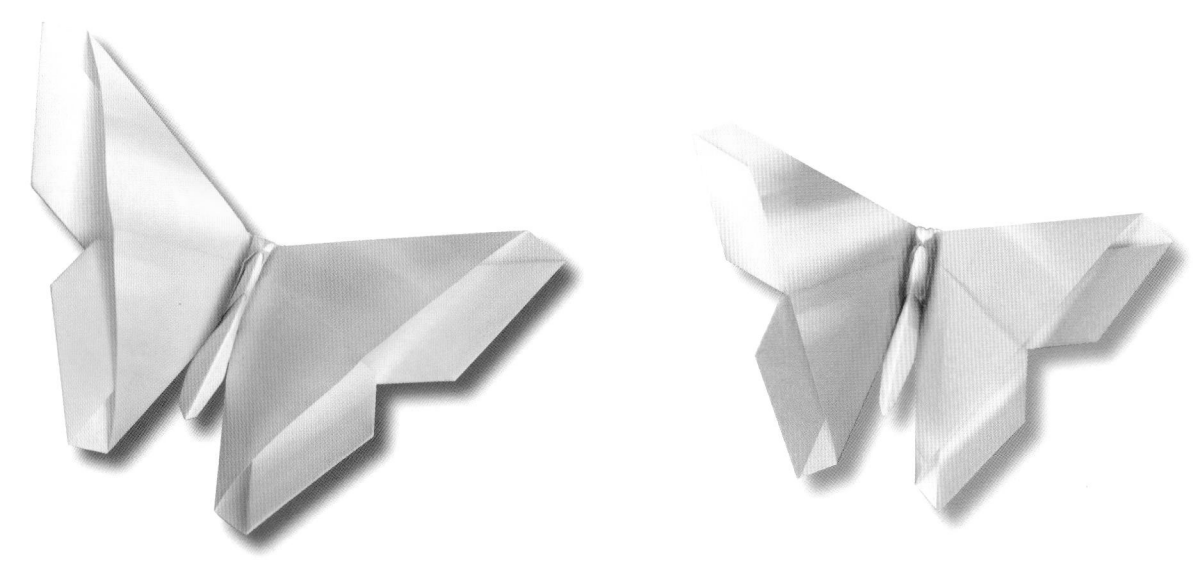

A Butterfly for Tony Cheng

"Cheng's Viceroy"

This design is named for our longtime friend, Tony Cheng; Origami USA Board member, folder, creator, teacher, and tireless origami enthusiast. He came up with this variation of "The Alice," and so we named it for him.

You'll most likely find "Cheng's Viceroy" feeding on a red hot chili pepper plant! Whether or not you can take the heat, he will be your steady friend. Witty and smart, kind and courageous, "Cheng's Viceroy" also guards the Gold Mine and manages its riches, harvesting donations and surplus materials once each year at the New York Convention for the benefit of the swarm.

> *safely pile it here*
> *mounds of unwanted treasure*
> *Gold Mine of Friendship*

This "Cheng's Viceroy" design will introduce a special wing modification of "The Alice."

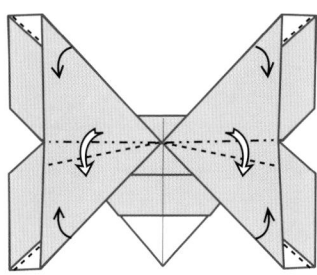

1. Begin with the "Butterfly for Alice Base" (pages 35 and 36, steps 1–13). Form a crimped overlap at the middle of each wing, by forming new leading edges while rolling the top edges and the bottom edges of each wing towards the center. (The excess paper rises along the center crease.) Use that mountain ridge to form an edge, folding the forewing paper down over the upper part of the hindwing, creating overlap.

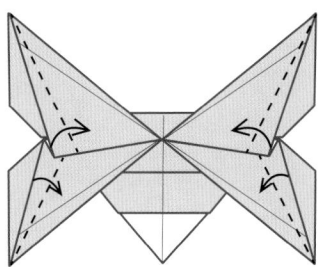

2. Your paper should look like this. Valley-fold the indicated edges inward, forming a color "V" pattern on each wing.

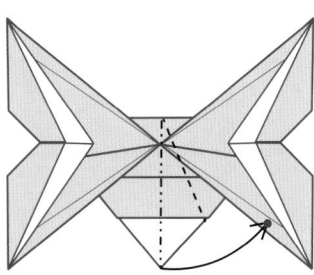

3. Mountain- and valley-fold the abdomen over the right wing.

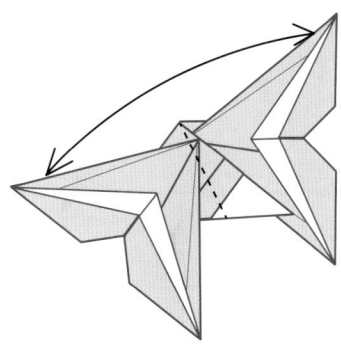

4. Valley-fold the left wing to match the right wing. Unfold.

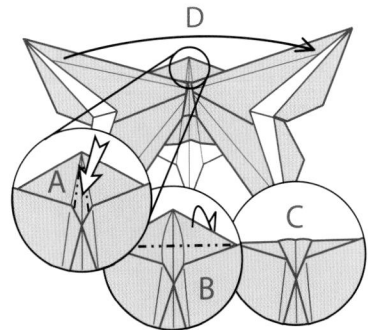

5. (A) Squash-fold the paper for the head. (B) Mountain-fold the corner behind. (C) Your paper should look like this. (D) Fold the wings together.

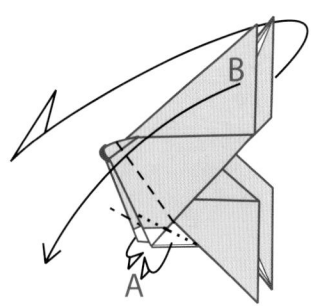

6. (A) Mountain-fold the abdomen edges inside. (B) Valley-fold the wings down on each side.

A Butterfly for Tony Cheng.

A Butterfly for Jane Winchell

"The Janey"

This butterfly is named for the Sara Fraser Robbins Director of the Art and Nature Center at the Peabody Essex Museum in Salem, Massachusetts. Janey also curates special exhibitions held at the center, and was responsible for "Origami Now!", a show co-curated by Michael LaFosse. It featured cutting-edge origami art on public display from June, 2007 through June, 2008.

Our "Janey" loves her job immensely, and loves her family even more. She is bright, learned, and warmhearted, and guides others along the right path to become the same.

is creased paper art?
there is no easy answer
I'll know when I see!

This design introduces the impact of reversing the flaps of the "Butterfly for Alice Base." There are two versions of hindwing details to differentiate the male from the female.

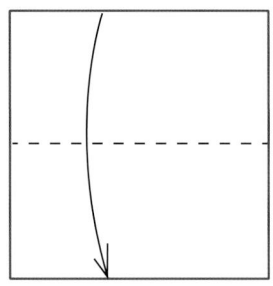

1. Valley-fold in half, top edge to bottom edge.

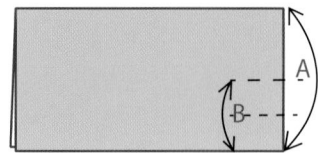

2. (A) Move the bottom edge of the top layer to the folded edge, above, and make a short pinch mark. Unfold. (B) Move the bottom edge of the top layer to the pinch mark edge and make another short pinch mark. Unfold.

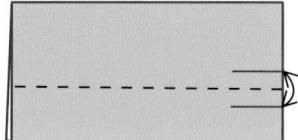

3. Lay the lower pinch mark on top of the upper pinch mark to valley-fold a crease halfway between the two pinch marks, all along the width, forming a flap 3/16 of the square. Unfold.

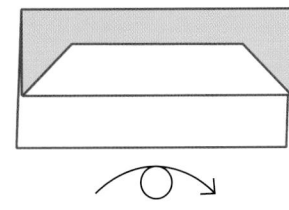

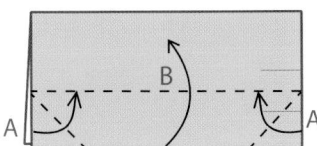

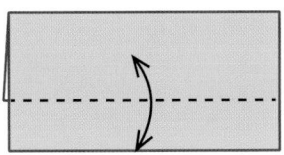

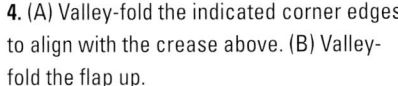

4. (A) Valley-fold the indicated corner edges to align with the crease above. (B) Valley-fold the flap up.

5. Turn over, left to right.

6. Valley-fold the bottom edge up, flush to the folded edge, behind. Unfold.

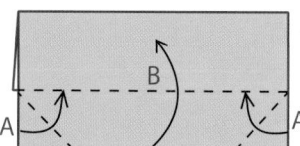

7. (A) Valley-fold the indicated corner edges to align with the crease above. (B) Valley-fold the flap up.

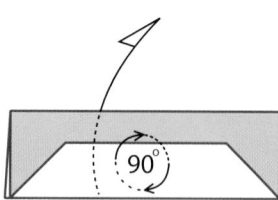

8. Open the paper and rotate 90 degrees.

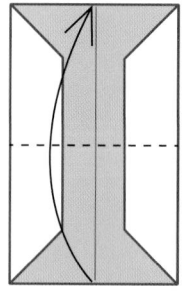

9. Your paper should look like this. Valley-fold the bottom edge to the top.

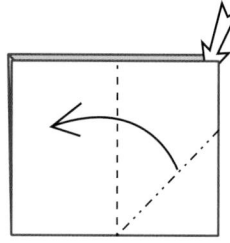

10. Squash-fold the right half. Look ahead to see results.

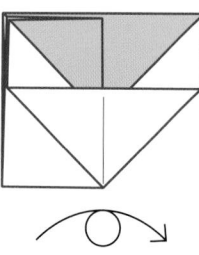

11. Your paper should look like this. Turn over, left to right.

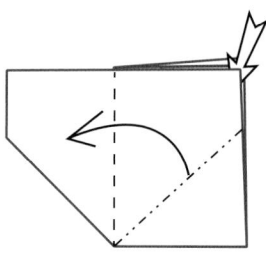

12. Squash-fold the right half.

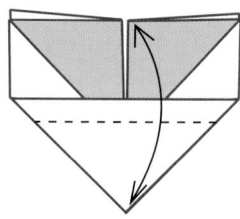

13. Valley-fold the bottom corner to the top of the split. Unfold.

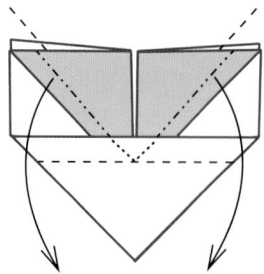

14. One at a time, squash-fold the right and left halves to form the wings. Look ahead at step 14 to see the shape.

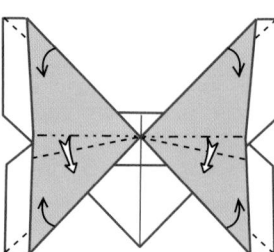

15. Form a crimped overlap at the middle of each wing, by rolling the top edges and the bottom edges of each wing towards the center. (The excess paper pushes up the center mountain crease to form an edge.) Fold the forewing paper down over the hindwing, creating the forewing overlap.

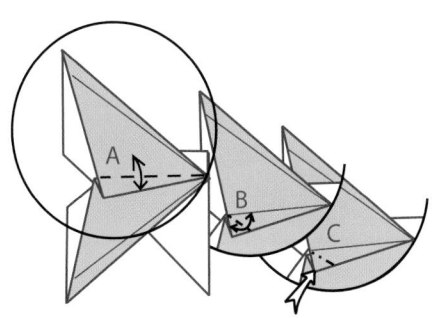

16. (A) Valley-fold the indicated flap up and down. (B) Valley-fold the short edge of the corner to the crease. (C) Inside-reverse-fold the corner. Repeat on the other wing.

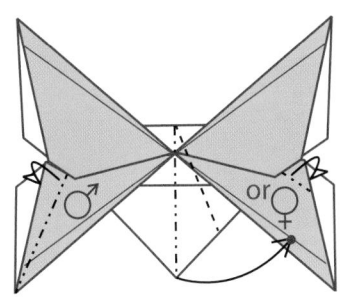

17. Your paper should look like this. Mountain-fold the indicated edges of the hindwings behind. Choose either the female or the male form at this stage. Mountain- and valley-fold the abdomen over the right wing.

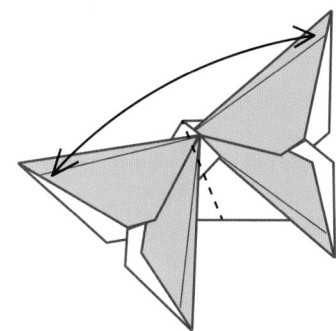

18. Valley-fold the left wing to match the right wing. Unfold.

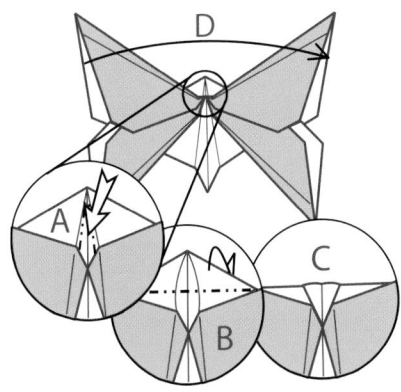

19. (A) Squash-fold the paper for the head. (B) Mountain-fold the corner behind. (C) Your paper should look like this. (D) Fold the wings together.

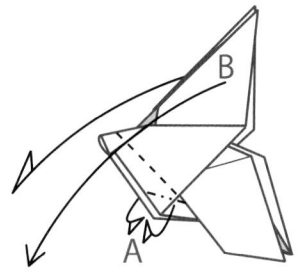

20. (A) Mountain-fold the lower abdomen edges inside. (B) Valley-fold the wings down on each side.

A Butterfly for Jane Winchell.

A Butterfly for Jan Polish

"The Jan"

This design is named for our longtime leader at Origami USA; a folder, designer, and facilitator who's carrying on the traditions of Lillian Oppenheimer through her extensive travels and superb teaching skills.

"The Jan" is our resourceful rock that we all count on for instant answers.

> *come gather around*
> *it takes many for lifting*
> *see what we have done!*

This design will introduce you to the effect achieved by *not* beveling the margins' corners, while keeping them on the outside instead of tucking them in. It also introduces a framed wing treatment that we love to use for showcasing fancy papers with a restrained contrasting border.

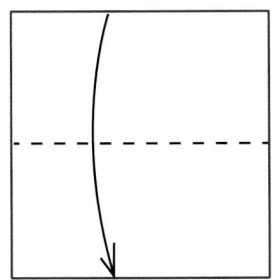

1. Valley-fold in half, top edge to bottom edge.

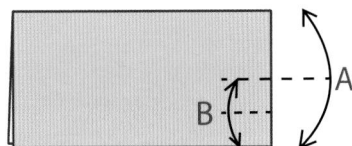

2. (A) Move the bottom edge of the top layer to the folded edge, above, and make a short pinch mark. Unfold. (B) Move the bottom edge of the top layer to the pinch mark edge and make a short pinch mark. Unfold.

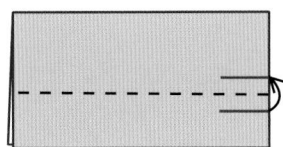

3. Lay the lower pinch mark on top of the upper pinch mark to valley-fold a flap 3/16ths of the square, all along the width, halfway between the two pinch marks.

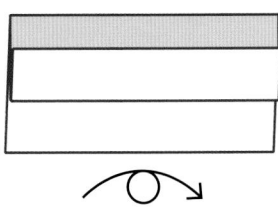

4. Turn over, left to right.

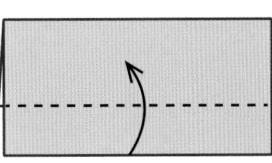

5. Valley-fold the bottom edge up, flush to the folded edge, behind.

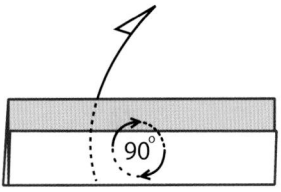

6. Open the paper and rotate 90 degrees.

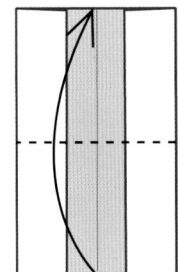

7. Your paper should look like this. Valley-fold the bottom edge to the top.

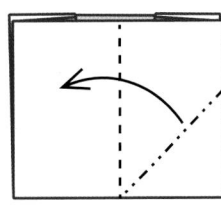

8. Squash-fold the right half. Look ahead to see results.

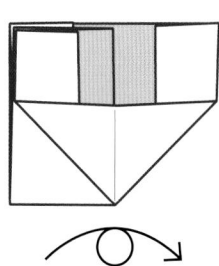

9. Your paper should look like this. Turn over, left to right.

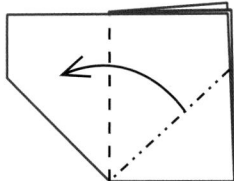

10. Squash-fold the right half.

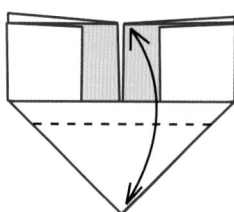

11. Valley-fold the bottom corner to the top of the split. Unfold.

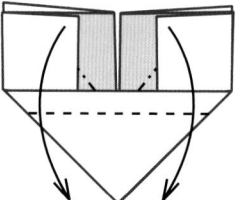

12. One at a time, squash-fold the right and left halves of the model to form the wings. Look ahead at step 13 for the results.

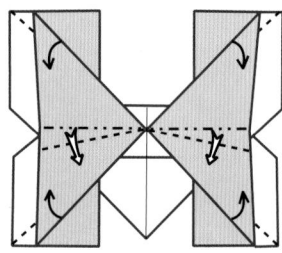

13. Form a crimped overlap at the middle of each wing by rolling the top edges and the bottom edges of each wing towards the center. (The excess paper pushes up the center mountain crease to form an edge.) Fold the forewing paper down over the hindwing, creating the forewing overlap.

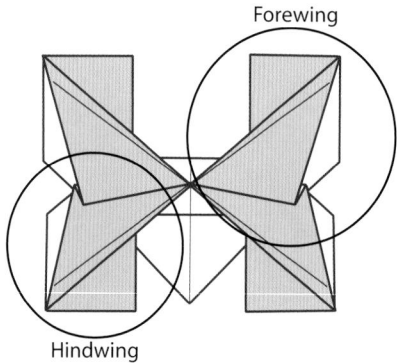

Forewing

Hindwing

14. Your paper should look like this.

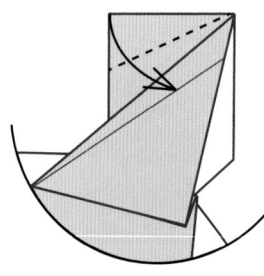

15. Valley-fold the top corners of the forewings to touch the crease line.

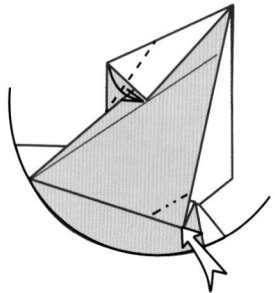

16. Valley-fold the new top corners of the forewings to the crease. Inside-reverse-fold the square corners to form the left and right wing notches.

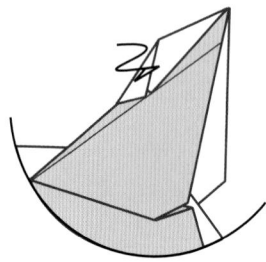

17. Tuck the raw edges of the top shape under the leading edges of each forewing.

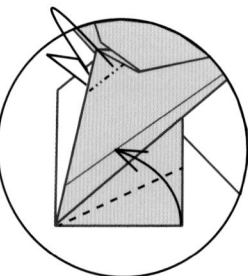

18. Mountain-fold the upper corner of the hindwings behind. Valley-fold the bottom corner of the hindwings to touch the crease line.

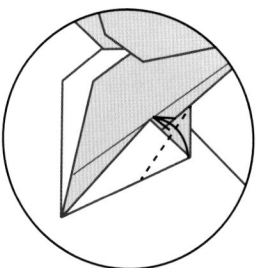

19. Valley-fold the new bottom corner to the crease for each hindwing.

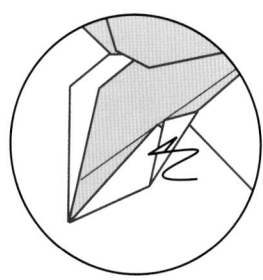

20. Tuck the raw edges of the top shape under the trailing edges of each hindwing.

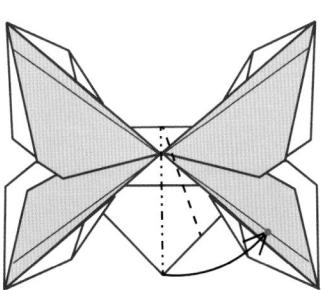

21. Mountain- and valley-fold the abdomen over the right wing.

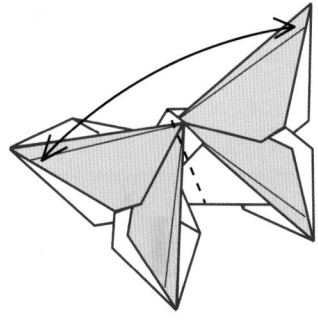

22. Valley-fold the left wing to match the right wing. Unfold.

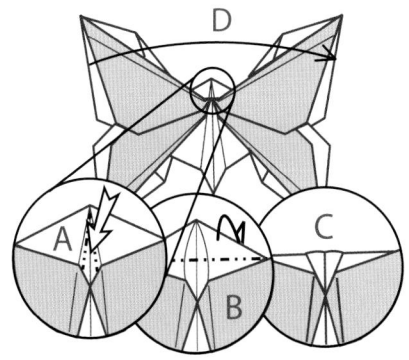

23. (A) Squash-fold the paper for the head. (B) Mountain-fold the corner behind. (C) Your paper should look like this. (D) Fold the wings together.

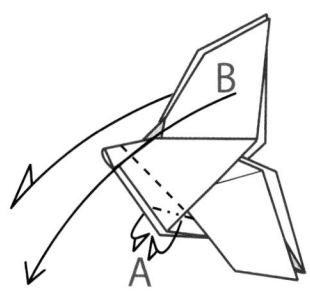

24. (A) Mountain-fold the abdomen edges inside. (B) Valley-fold the wings down on each side.

A Butterfly for Jan Polish.

A Butterfly for Mr. Makoto Yamaguchi

"The Makoto Cho"

This butterfly is named for Mr. Makoto Yamaguchi, "Gallery Origami House" founder, author, origami designer and publisher. Mr. Yamaguchi is the beloved mentor and chief organizer of publications by wonderfully advanced, "supercomplex" origami designers and folders in Japan and throughout the world.

> *my youngest folders*
> *are quite talented indeed!*
> *how far will they go?*

This design will introduce staggered flaps and an Aztec wing. It also features a special hindwing detail obtained by folding a Rabbit's Ear, and so we call it a Rabbit Spot!

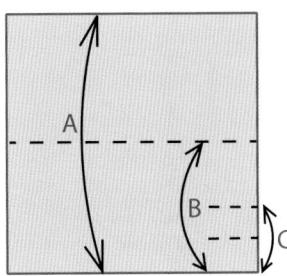

1. (A) Valley-fold in half, bottom edge to top. Unfold. (B) Move the bottom edge to the center crease and make a short pinch mark. Unfold. (C) Move the bottom edge to the pinch mark and make a short pinch mark. Unfold.

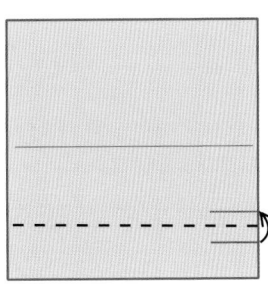

2. Lay the lower pinch mark on top of the upper pinch mark and valley-fold all the way across the paper.

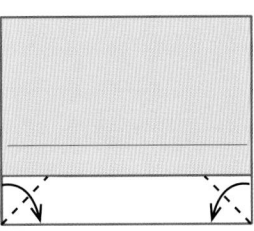

3. Valley-fold the indicated edges to align with the bottom folded edge.

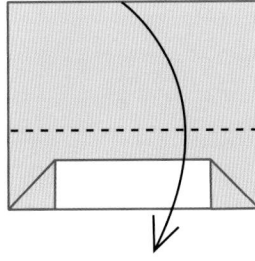

4. Use the horizontal crease to valley-fold the top edge down.

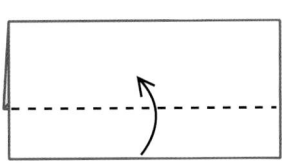

5. Valley-fold the bottom edge up, flush to the folded edge, behind.

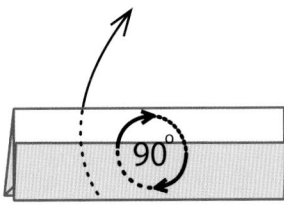

6. Open the paper and rotate 90 degrees.

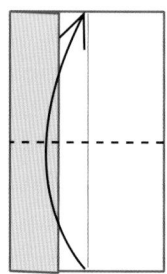

7. Your paper should look like this. Valley-fold the bottom edge to the top.

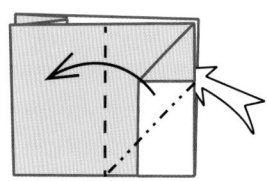

8. Squash-fold the right half. Look ahead to see results.

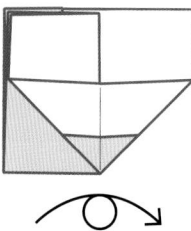

9. Your paper should look like this. Turn over, left to right.

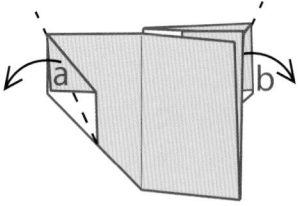

10. Pull out and flatten flaps "a" and "b."

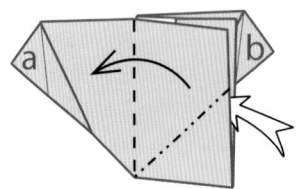

11. Squash-fold.

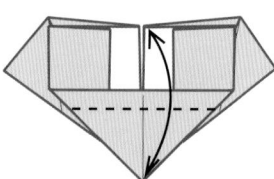

12. Valley-fold the bottom corner to the top of the split. Unfold.

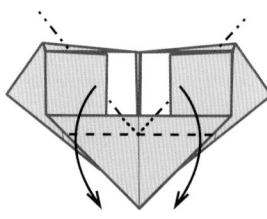

13. One at a time, squash-fold the right and left halves of the model to form the wings. Look ahead at step 14 to see the results.

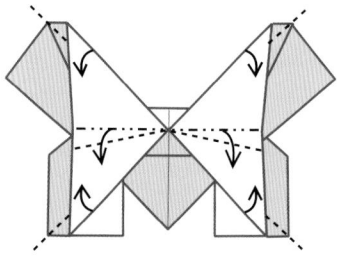

14. Form a crimped overlap at the middle of each wing, by rolling the top edges and the bottom edges of each wing towards the center. (The excess paper pushes up the center mountain crease to form an edge.) Fold the forewing paper down over the hindwing, creating the forewing overlap.

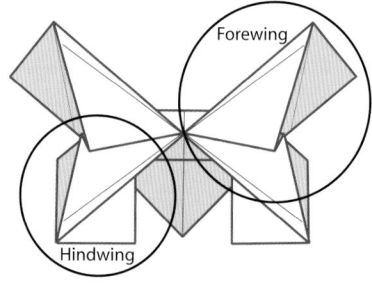

15. Your paper should look like this.

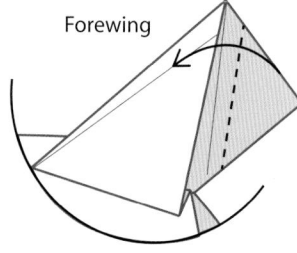

16. Valley-fold the square corner of each forewing so that the top edge runs parallel to the crease.

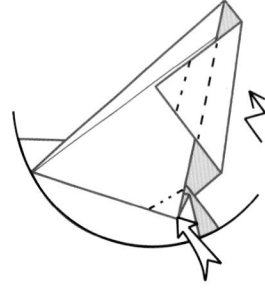

17. Mountain- and valley-fold the triangle flap into thirds of each forewing. Inside-reverse fold the lower corner of each forewing.

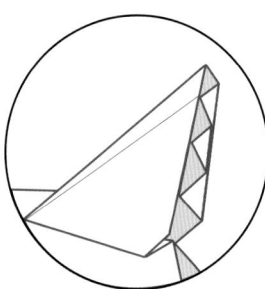

18. Your paper should look like this.

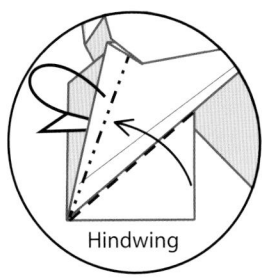

19. Mountain-fold the outside edge behind for both hindwings. Valley-fold the triangle flap over each hindwing.

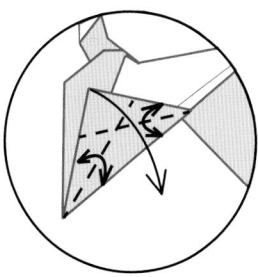

20. One at a time, valley-fold and unfold the free edges of the triangle to the bottom, folded edge.

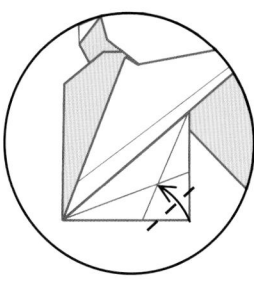

21. Valley-fold the corner to the intersection of creases.

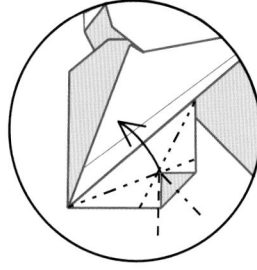

22. Form a "Rabbit Ear" and the "Rabbit Ear Spot": Use the creases to collapse the flap on top of each hindwing. Look ahead for the shape. Notice that the colored triangle will be folded in half.

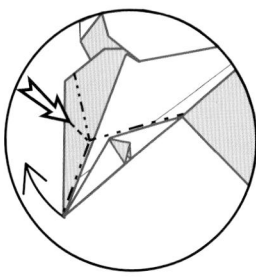

23. Mountain-fold the wing corner in half, and fold flat to the back side, pointing away from the body.

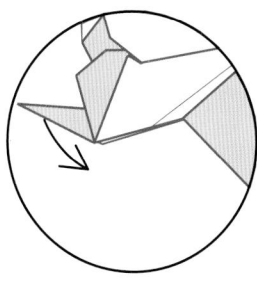

24. Open. Look ahead for the shape.

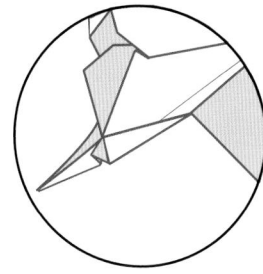

25. The completed hindwing.

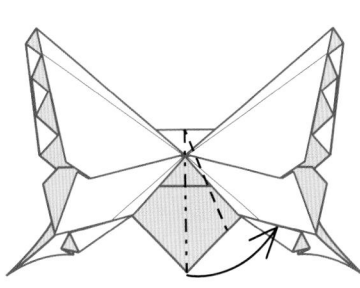

26. Mountain- and valley-fold the abdomen over the right wing.

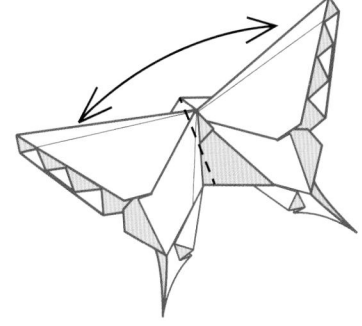

27. Valley-fold the left wing to match the right wing. Unfold.

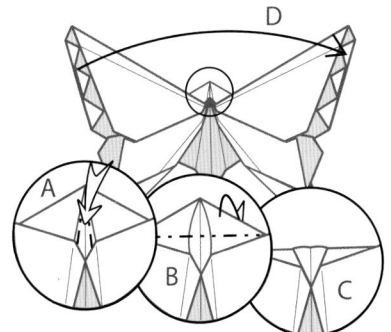

28. (A) Squash-fold paper for the head. (B) Mountain-fold the corner behind. (C) Your paper should look like this. (D) Fold the wings together.

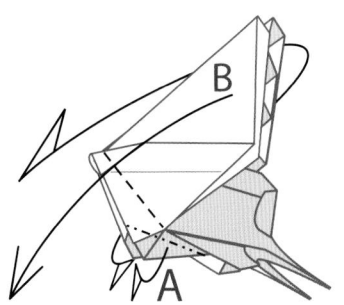

29. (A) Mountain-fold the abdomen edges inside. (B) Valley-fold the wings down on each side.

A Butterfly for Mr. Makoto Yamaguchi.

A Butterfly for Vanessa Gould

"The Vanessa"

This design is named for Vanessa Gould, Peabody Award-winning filmmaker and author of *Between the Folds*, an engaging documentary presenting the state of the art of origami, its artists, mathematicians, and engineers, collectively moving the body of folding knowledge forward.

"The Vanessa" is our beloved storyteller. She flies around the world probing thoughts, gathering insight. Friends we thought we knew, we realized we barely knew. She constructs her story logically, and wraps ideas in a cocoon until we have thought about them long enough. Her story emerges bearing wings, and viewers don't just understand origami, they fall in love with it. "The Vanessa" slips into screening rooms, movie theaters, TV sets, and computer screens everywhere, telling truth and beauty, magic and wonder. Through her perseverance, remarkable courage, and selfless sacrifice, she makes it cool for kids to question, think, work hard, and explore.

seven minutes planned...
behold this visible math!
oh, my God! A Peabody!

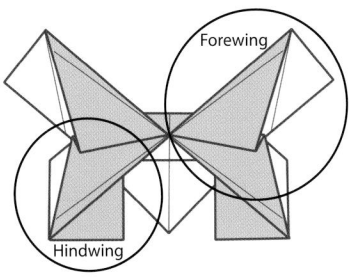

1. Begin with the butterfly base from step 15 of "A Butterfly for Mr. Makoto Yamaguchi" (page 48).

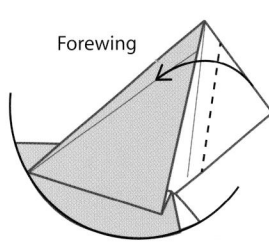

2. Valley-fold the square corner of each forewing so that the top edge runs parallel to the crease.

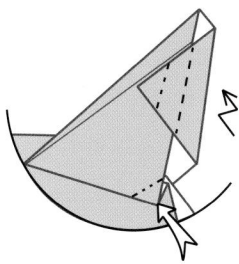

3. Mountain- and valley-fold the triangle flap of each forewing into thirds. Inside-reverse-fold the lower corner of each forewing.

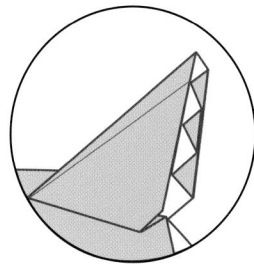

4. Your paper should look like this.

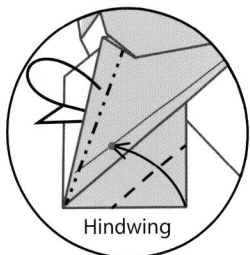

5. For each hindwing, mountain-fold the outside edge behind. Valley-fold the tip of the triangle flap to touch the crease.

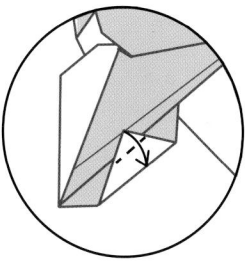

6. For each hindwing, valley-fold the tip of the triangle flap to touch the folded edge.

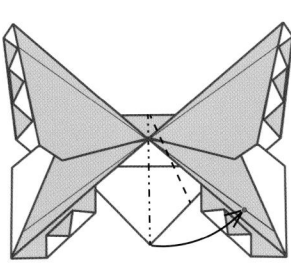

7. Mountain- and valley-fold the abdomen over the right wing.

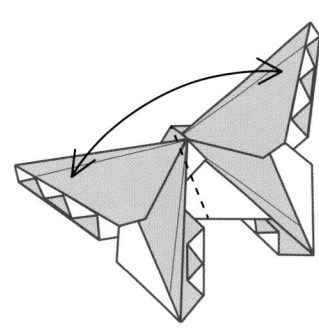

8. Valley-fold the left wing to match the right wing. Unfold.

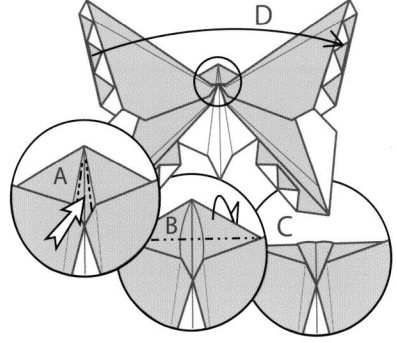

9. (A) Squash-fold the paper for the head. (B) Mountain-fold the corner behind. (C) Your paper should look like this. (D) Fold the wings together.

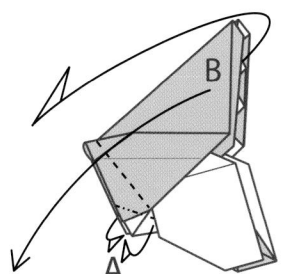

10. (A) Mountain-fold the abdomen edges inside. (B) Valley-fold the wings down on each side.

A Butterfly for Vanessa Gould.

A Butterfly for Robert Lang

"The Lang"

The *Papilio appalachiensis* (Appalachian Tiger Swallowtail) butterfly was the real world inspiration for this model.

Photo by Joe Mueller. (Source: *http://upload. wikimedia.org/wikipedia/commons/1/1a/P_ app_m_holotype_dorsal.jpg*)

This butterfly is named for Robert Lang, a LASER optics physicist, engineer, designer, author, and artist—best known for bridging the gap between disciplines—who is also a Board member of Origami USA. His work makes artists' origami more thoughtful and planned, while coaxing engineers to make their origami a bit more artful.

And so the "The Lang" butterfly is our Senior Science Officer, the logical, rational, even-tempered arbiter of all that is too complex for mere mortals.

> *if it can be done*
> *I'll enjoy all the hard work*
> *it will be so cool!*

This design will introduce another style of thorax, as well as the "prongtail" hindwing.

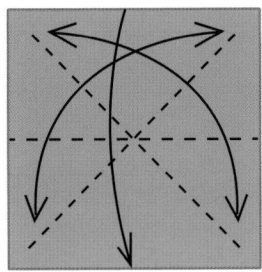

1. Begin with the prominent color you desire face up. Valley-fold in half diagonally, both ways, unfolding after each. Do not fold all the way through to the corners. Valley-fold in half, top edge to bottom.

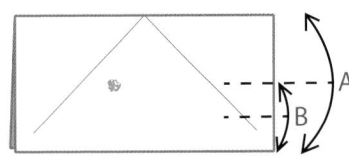

2. (A) Move the bottom edge of the top layer to the center crease and make a short pinch mark. Unfold. (B) Move the bottom edge to the pinch mark and make a short pinch mark. Unfold.

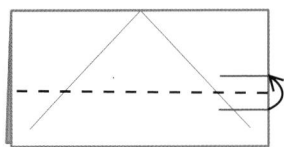

3. Lay the lower pinch mark upon the upper pinch mark and valley-fold all the way across the paper.

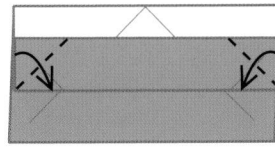

4. Valley-fold the indicated edges of the corners to align with the folded edge.

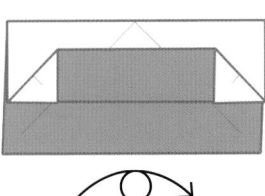

5. Turn over, left to right.

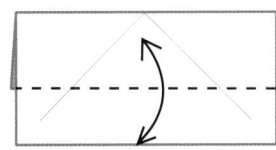

6. Valley-fold the bottom edge up at the level of the folded edge, behind. Unfold.

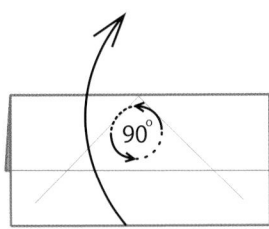

7. Open the front layer of the paper and rotate 90 degrees counterclockwise.

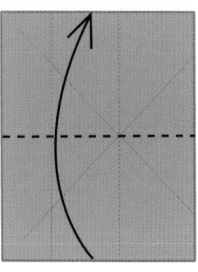

8. The folded edge should be on the right. Valley-fold bottom edge to top.

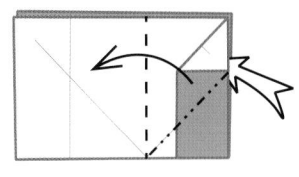

9. Squash-fold the right segment of the paper.

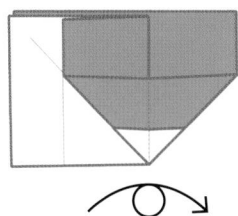

10. Your paper should look like this. Turn over, left to right.

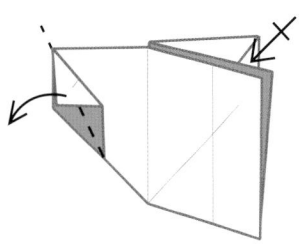

11. Pull open the indicated flaps and flatten.

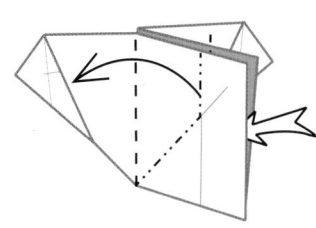

12. Squash-fold.

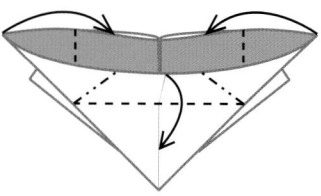

13. Use the horizontal crease of the front layer to valley-fold the top edge down, while folding the left and right corners in as a squash-fold. Look ahead at step 14 for the shape.

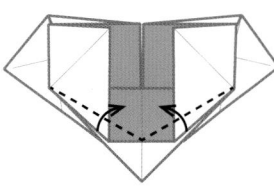

14. Valley-fold the left and right edges of the front flap up, forming a point at the bottom of the flap.

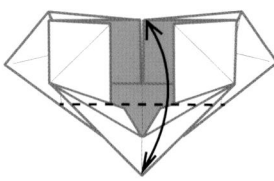

15. Valley-fold the bottom corner to the top of the split, Unfold.

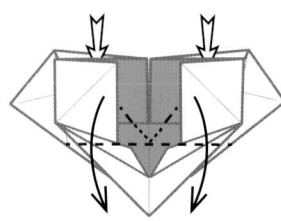

16. One at a time, squash-fold the right and left halves of the model to form the wings. Look ahead at Step 17.

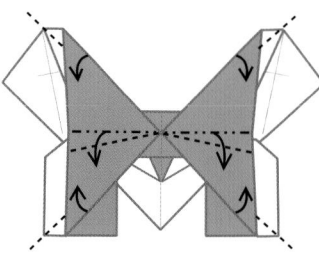

17. Form a crimped overlap at the middle of each wing, by rolling the top edges and the bottom edges of each wing towards the center. (The excess paper pushes up the center mountain crease to form an edge.) Fold the forewing paper down over the hindwing, creating the forewing overlap.

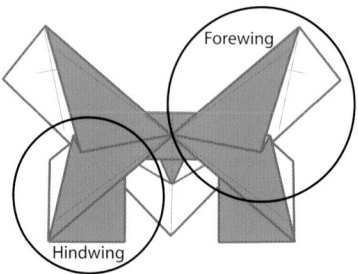

18. Your paper should look like this.

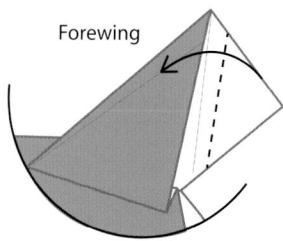

19. On both forewings, valley-fold the square corner so that the top edge runs parallel to the crease.

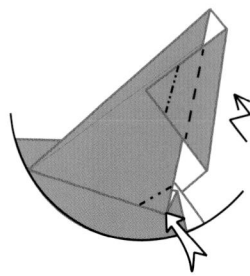

20. Mountain and valley-fold the triangle flap into thirds. Inside-reverse fold the lower corner of the forewing.

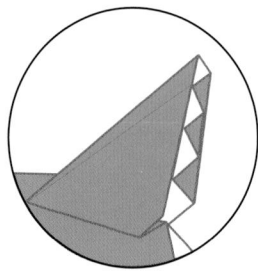

21. Your paper should look like this.

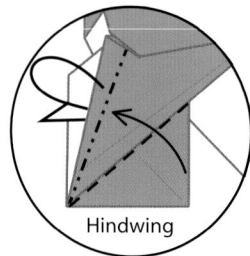

22. On both hindwings, mountain-fold the outside edge behind. Valley-fold the triangle flap over the hindwing.

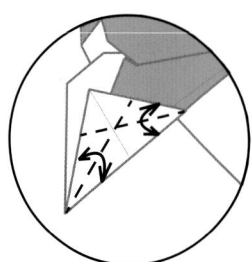

23. One at a time, valley-fold and unfold the free edges of the triangle to the bottom folded edge.

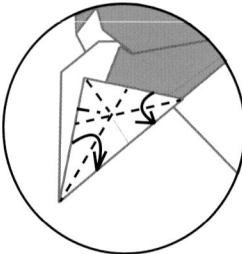

24. Form a "Rabbit Ear": Use the creases to fold the square corner in half while collapsing the flap on top of the hindwing. Look ahead for the shape.

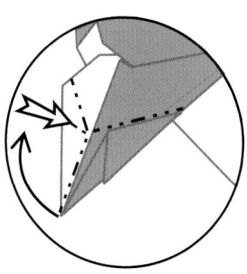

25. Mountain-fold the wing corner in half and fold flat to the back side, pointing away from the body.

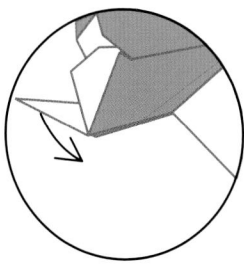

26. Move the folded point back towards the body and make a graceful shape.

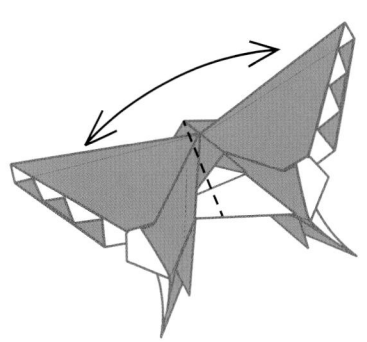

27. The completed "Prongtail" hindwing.

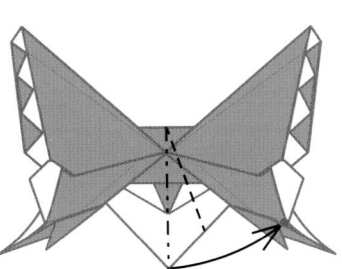

28. Mountain- and valley-fold the abdomen over the right wing.

29. Valley-fold the left wing to match the right wing. Unfold.

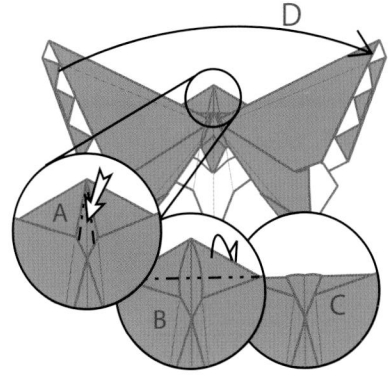

30. (A) Squash-fold the paper for the head. (B) Mountain-fold the corner behind. (C) Your paper should look like this. (D) Fold the wings together.

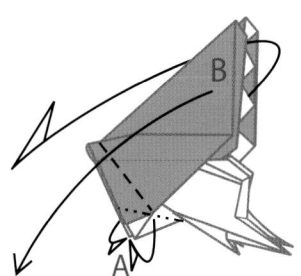

31. (A) Mountain-fold the abdomen edges inside. (B) Valley-fold the wings down on each side.

A Butterfly for Robert Lang.

A Butterfly for Emiko Kruckner

"The Emiko Fritillary"

This butterfly is named for the late Emiko Kruckner, a Yoshizawa student and liaison between Master Yoshizawa and Michael LaFosse. She arranged Michael's first trip to Tokyo in 1995, to advance the understanding of Yoshizawa's importance in the art world.

   "The Emiko Fritillary" is our gracious Cultural Ambassador in the kimono, skillfully straddling cultures to promote friendship through communication and understanding.

the Mystery Man
captured your admiration
now feel his impact

This design will introduce a wing shape reminiscent of that of a cherry blossom, and so we call it the *sakura* style.

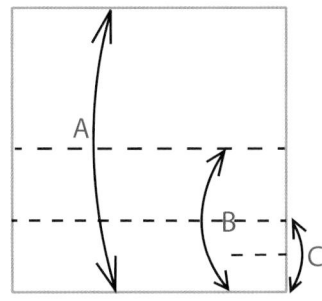

1. Begin with the minor color facing up. (A) Valley-fold in half, bottom edge to top. Unfold. (B) Valley-fold the bottom edge to the center crease. Unfold. (C) Move the bottom edge to the lower crease line and make a pinch mark. Unfold.

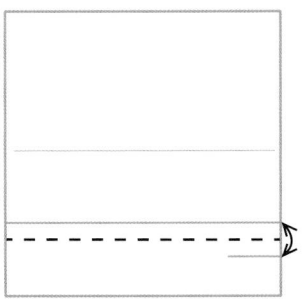

2. Lay the lower pinch mark on top of the lower full crease above it and valley-fold all the way across the paper. Unfold.

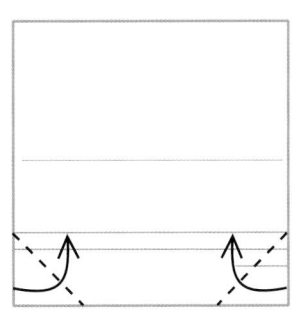

3. Valley-fold the bottom corners up to align with crease "B" from step 1.

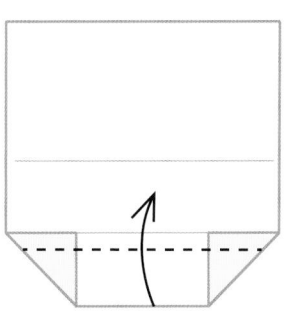

4. Valley-fold the bottom edge up using the crease formed in step 2.

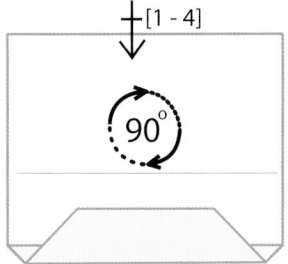

5. Repeat steps 1–4 with the opposite edge. Rotate the paper 90 degrees.

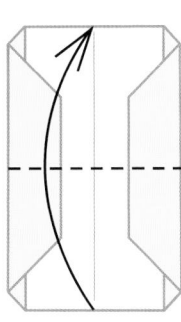

6. Valley-fold the bottom edge to the top.

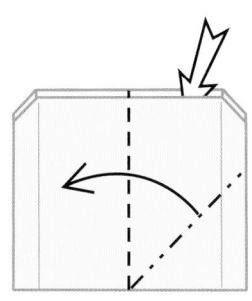

7. Squash-fold the right half.

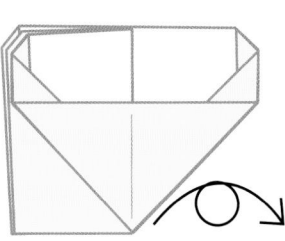

8. Your paper should look like this. Turn over, left to right.

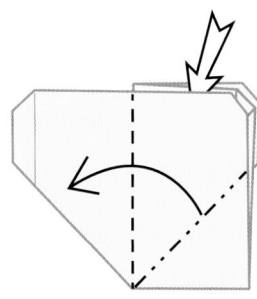

9. Squash-fold.

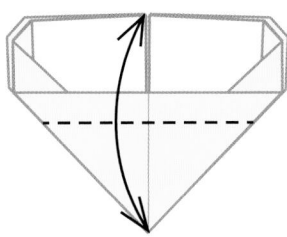

10. Valley-fold the bottom corner to the top of the split. Unfold.

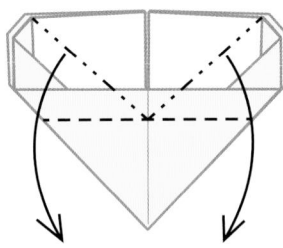

11. One at a time, squash-fold the upper right and left halves of the model, forming the wings.

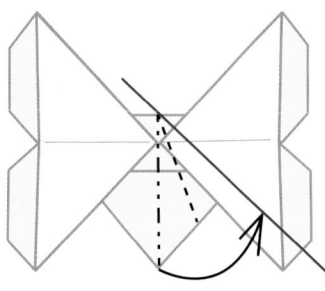

12. Mountain- and valley-fold the abdomen over the right wing.

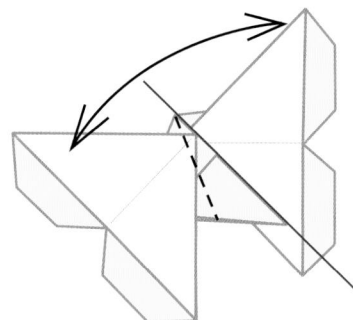

13. Valley-fold the left wing to match the right wing. Unfold.

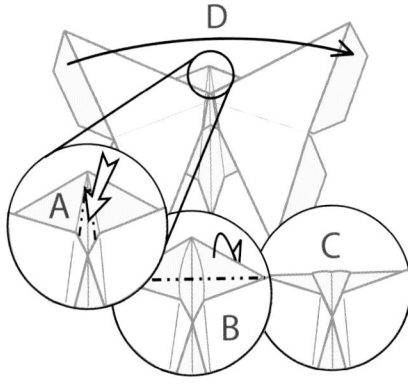

14. (A) Squash-fold the paper for the head. (B) Mountain-fold the corner behind. (C) Your paper should look like this. (D) Fold the wings together.

15. (A) Mountain-fold the abdomen edges inside. (B) Valley-fold the wings down on each side.

The Butterfly for Emiko Kruckner. Now try a couple of variations.

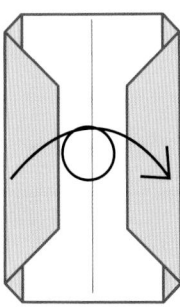

1. Fold through to step 6. Turn over, left to right.

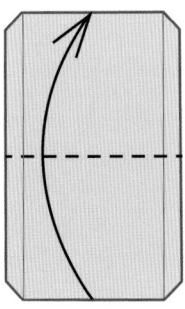

2. Valley-fold the bottom edge to the top, and then complete the rest of the folding sequence.

A Butterfly for Emiko Kruckner, Variation I.

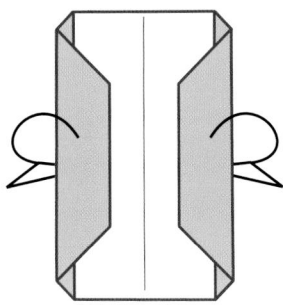

1. Fold through to step 6. Reverse the front flaps to the back.

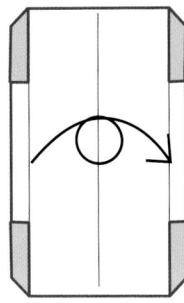

2. Turn over, left to right.

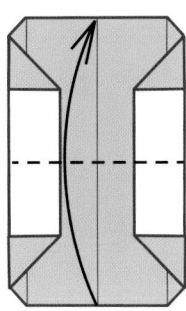

3. Valley-fold the bottom edge to the top, and then complete the rest of the folding sequence.

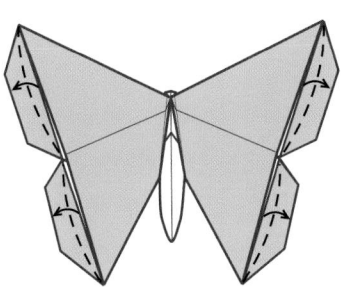

4. Valley-fold the free edges on the outer-most top layers to form *lunules*.

A Butterfly for Emiko Kruckner, Variation II.

A Butterfly for Kyoko Kondo

"The Kyoko"

This design is named for Kyoko Kondo, origami artist, teacher, organizer, and tireless volunteer, serving New York, Boston, and Hawaii-based folders.

"The Kyoko" is our power plant, our dynamo, as well as our smiling and confident supporter. She knows the best way, and does much of the hard work. Working beside her guarantees immense accomplishment.

helping is the way
of loving your cherished friends!
we are truly blessed!

This design will introduce a hybrid design, borrowing the pleasing combination of the forewing from "The Alice" (page 34), and the hindwing from "The Emiko Fritillary" (page 58).

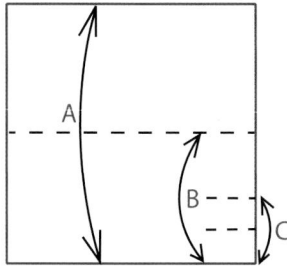

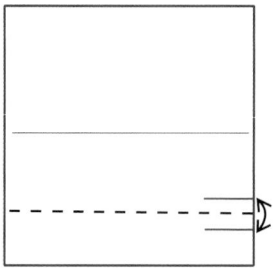

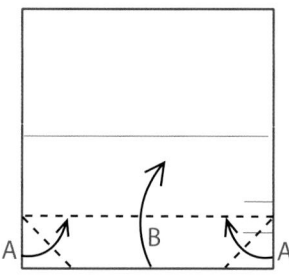

1. Begin with the minor color facing up. (A) Valley-fold in half, bottom edge to top. Unfold. (B) Valley-fold the bottom edge to the center crease and make a pinch mark. Unfold. (C) Move the bottom edge to the lower crease line and make a pinch mark. Unfold.

2. Lay the lower pinch mark on top of the upper pinch mark and valley-fold all the way across the paper. Unfold.

3. (A) Valley-fold the bottom corners up to align with the crease from step 2. (B) Use the same crease to valley-fold the bottom edge up.

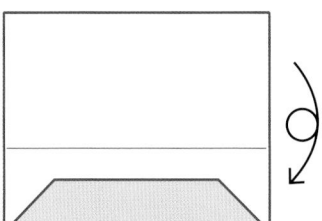

4. Turn over, top to bottom.

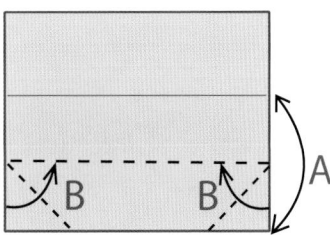

5. (A) Valley-fold the bottom edge to the crease. Unfold. (B) Valley-fold the bottom corners to the crease.

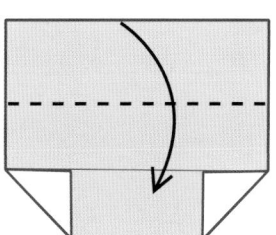

6. Use the upper crease to valley-fold the top edge down.

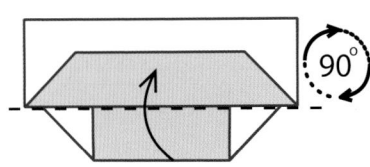

7. Valley-fold the bottom flap up and over the folded edge of the top layer. Rotate the paper 90 degrees clockwise.

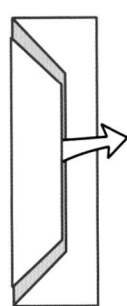

8. Open the paper.

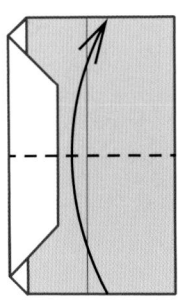

9. Valley-fold the bottom edge to the top.

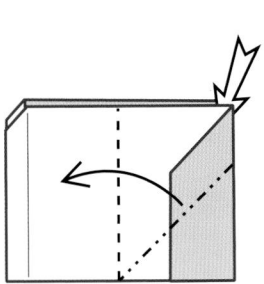

10. Squash-fold the right half.

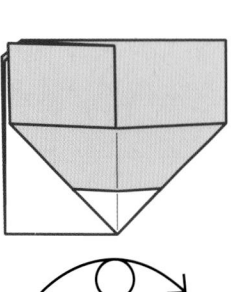

11. Your paper should look like this. Turn the paper over, left to right.

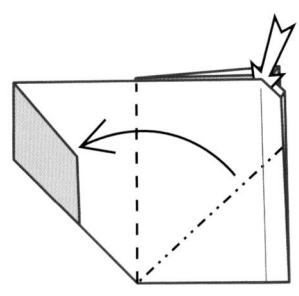

12. Squash-fold the right half.

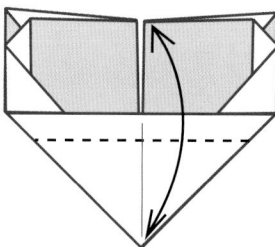

13. Valley-fold the bottom corner to the top of the split. Unfold.

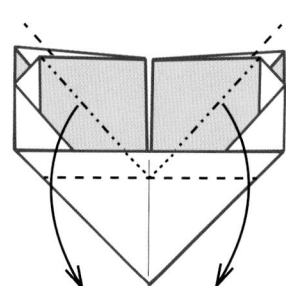

14. One at a time, squash-fold the upper right and left halves of the model, forming the wings.

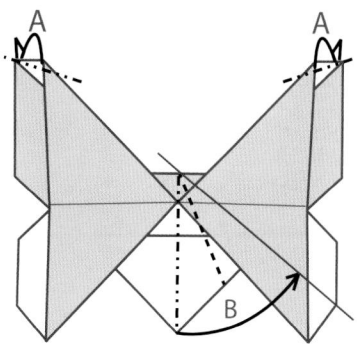

15. (A) Mountain-fold the top edges of the forewings behind. (B) Mountain- and valley-fold the abdomen over the right wing.

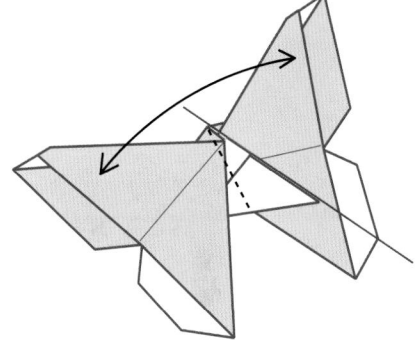

16. Valley-fold the left wing to match the right wing. Unfold.

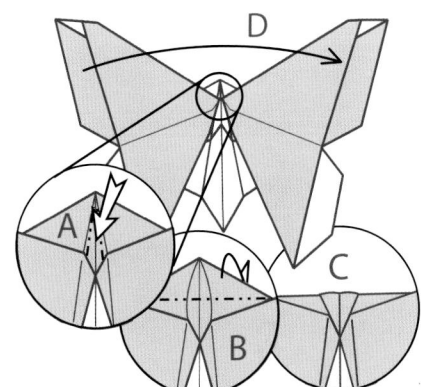

17. (A) Squash-fold the paper for the head. (B) Mountain-fold the corner behind. (C) Your paper should look like this. (D) Fold the wings together.

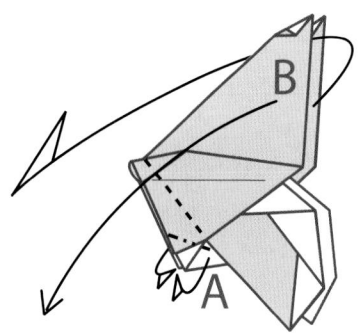

18. (A) Mountain-fold the abdomen edges inside. (B) Valley-fold the wings down on each side.

A Butterfly for Kyoko Kondo.

A Butterfly for Killian Mansfield

"The Killian"

This design is named for the late Killian Mansfield, a friendly soul we felt we had always known. This young, advanced origami enthusiast caused us to reflect on what is truly important. Diagnosed with a rare synovial cancer at age eleven, Killian endured operations, medications, and therapies, one after another, for much of his short life. Determined to experience all the living any normal young person enjoys, he kept learning and growing between visits to the experts. We met him only a few months before he passed, and were deeply moved by his enthusiasm and energy. He gave up playing the violin when it became too painful to hold it to his chin, and so he learned to strum the ukelele instead. Captivated by the wonder of art, he focused on blues music and advanced origami. He even cut a[n] ukelele blues CD, working with a host of famous blues musicians to help raise money to fight childhood cancers. Learn about the Killian Mansfield Foundation at *killianmansfield.org*.

When you fold "The Killian" you honor the child in us longing to be fully alive. Take advantage of today, and do something special for the other Killians fighting to be just like us!

to Doctor John's magic
fold, and listen peacefully
transcend all illness

This design will introduce an asymmetrical squash.

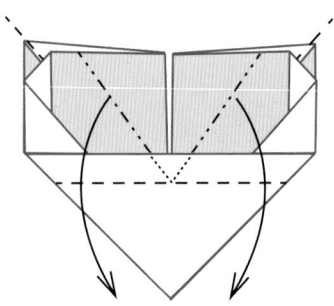

1. Fold through step 13 of "A Butterfly For Kyoko Kondo" (page 62). One at a time, squash-fold the upper right and left halves of the model, forming the wings. Notice that this squash is not symmetrical: the top-layer triangles are *scalene*.

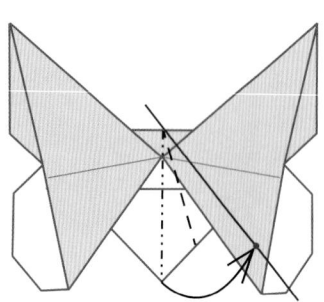

2. Mountain- and valley-fold the abdomen over the right wing.

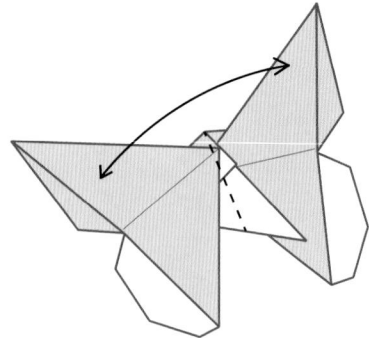

3. Valley-fold the left wing to match the right wing. Unfold.

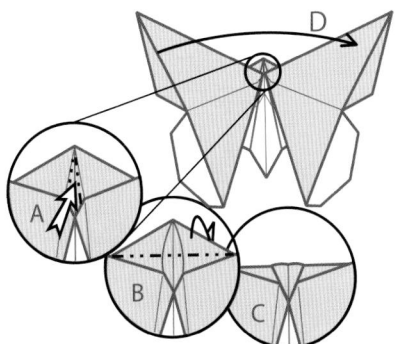

4. (A) Squash-fold the paper for the head. (B) Mountain-fold the corner behind. (C) Your paper should look like this. (D) Fold the wings together.

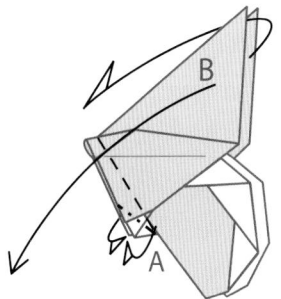

5. (A) Mountain-fold the abdomen edges inside. (B) Valley-fold the wings down on each side.

A Butterfly for Killian Mansfield.

A Butterfly for Eric Joisel

"The Joisel"

Named for the late Eric Joisel, Parisian sculptor turned origami master who stunned the origami world with his high level of technical and artistic achievement, this *Papillon pour Eric* embodies the spirit of our genius-artist-sculptor-clown.

He can make paper do anything, even fold itself. He travels the world, proclaiming himself "silly and stupid" while doing what no one else can even imagine doing. The "Butterfly for Eric" (*Papillon pour Eric*) elicits music from the gnomes, and lights the morning sky to make the paper rooster crow.

the "clay" in your hands
became thousands of folders
your hands warmed clay hearts!

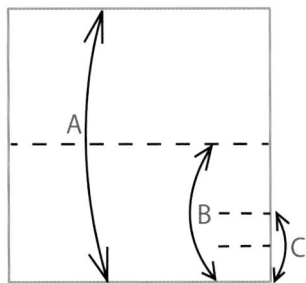

1. Begin with the minor color facing up. (A) Valley-fold in half, bottom edge to top. Unfold. (B) Valley-fold the bottom edge to the center crease and make a pinch mark. Unfold. (C) Move the bottom edge to the lower crease line and make a pinch mark. Unfold.

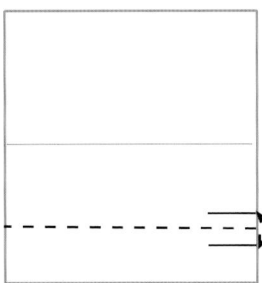

2. Lay the lower pinch mark on top of the upper pinch mark and valley-fold all the way across the paper. Unfold.

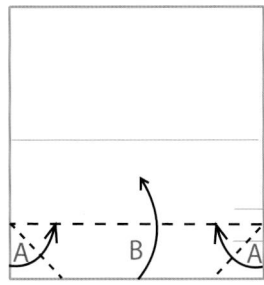

3. (A) Valley-fold the bottom corners up to align with the crease from step 2. (B) Use the same crease to valley-fold the bottom edge up.

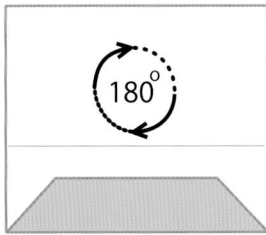

4. Rotate the paper 180 degrees.

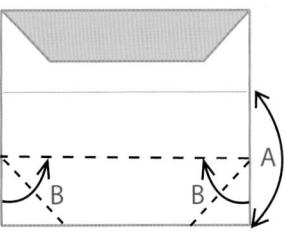

5. (A) Valley-fold the bottom edge to the crease. Unfold. (B) Valley-fold the bottom corners to the crease.

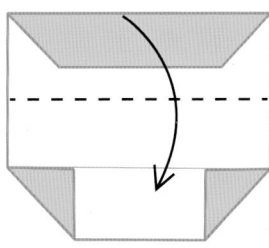

6. Use the upper crease to valley-fold the top edge down.

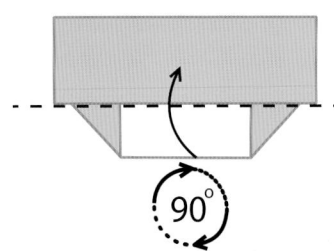

7. Valley-fold the bottom flap up and over the folded edge of the top layer. Rotate the paper 90 degrees clockwise.

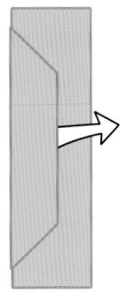

8. Open the paper.

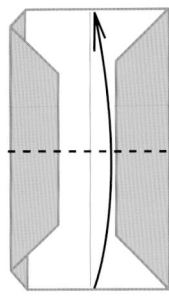

9. Valley-fold the bottom edge to the top.

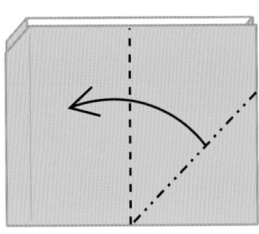

10. Squash-fold the right half.

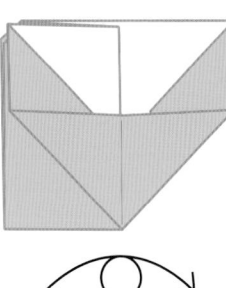

11. Your paper should look like this. Turn the paper over, left to right.

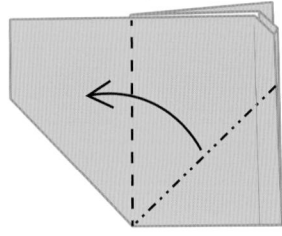

12. Squash-fold the right half.

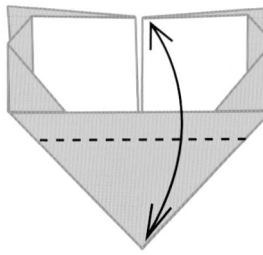

13. Valley-fold the bottom corner to the top of the split. Unfold.

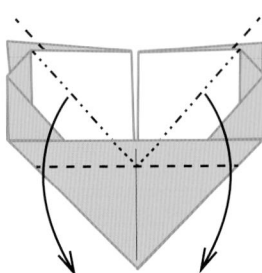

14. One at a time, squash-fold the upper right and left halves of the model, forming the wings.

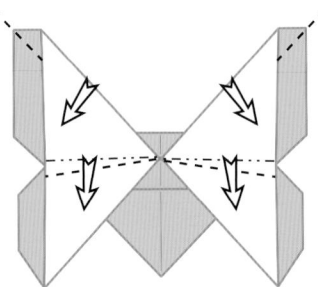

15. Move the top layer of the leading edge of the forewing down. Fold the mountain crease in the middle of the wing down, forming a wing overlap.

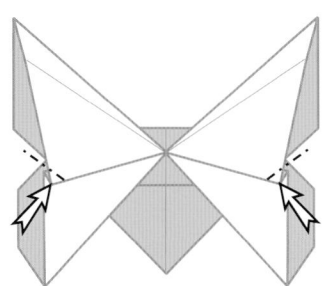

16. Inside-reverse fold the indicated corners.

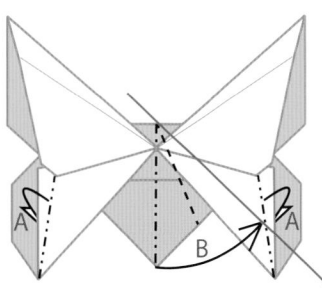

17. (A) Mountain-fold the indicated edges of the hindwings behind. (B) Mountain- and valley-fold the abdomen over the right wing.

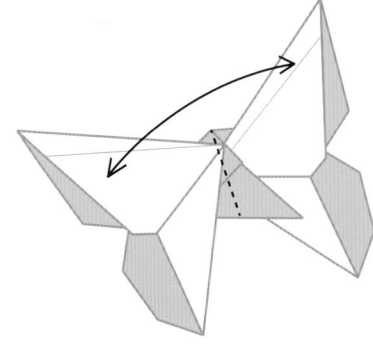

18. Valley-fold the left wing to match the right wing. Unfold.

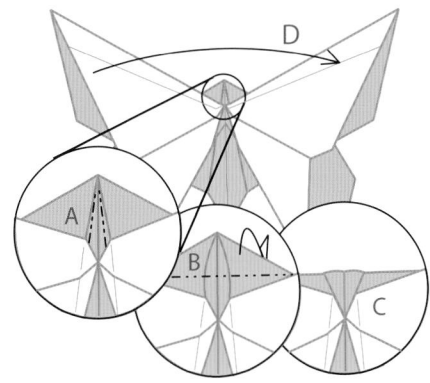

19. (A) Squash-fold the paper for the head. (B) Mountain-fold the corner behind. (C) Your paper should look like this. (D) Fold the wings together.

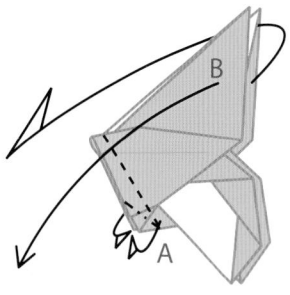

20. (A) Mountain-fold the abdomen edges inside. (B) Valley-fold the wings down on each side.

A Butterfly for Eric Joisel.

A Butterfly for Sok Song

"The Sok"

The *Limenitis arthemis* (White Admiral) butterfly was the real world inspiration for this model.

Photo by D. Gordon E. Robertson. (Source: *http://upload.wikimedia.org/wikipedia/commons/a/a9/White_Admiral.jpg*)

This design is named for Sok Song, designer and creator of *Creased* magazine, talented artist, author, folder, and friend.

"The Sok" is simply elegant. The clean lines and pleasing shapes transmit a no-nonsense message: We are not alone in the world. We are not hermits. It does matter how you look, and how you carry yourself. People notice!

black cat sits alone
eyes glowing, moonlight slivers
he works all night long!

This design will introduce the "Cat's Eye" pattern, and the artful use of the *lunule*.

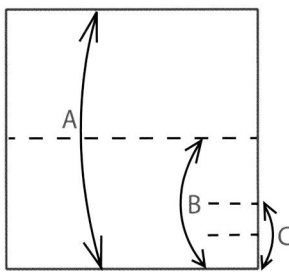

1. Begin with the minor color facing up. (A) Valley-fold in half, bottom edge to top. Unfold. (B) Valley-fold the bottom edge to the center crease and make a pinch mark. Unfold. (C) Move the bottom edge to the lower crease line and make a pinch mark. Unfold.

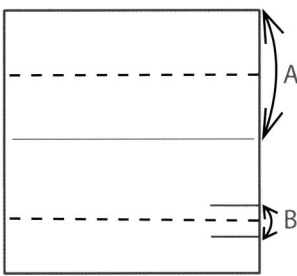

2. (A) Valley-fold the top edge to the center crease. Unfold. (B) Lay the lower pinch mark on top of the upper pinch mark and valley-fold all the way across the paper. Unfold.

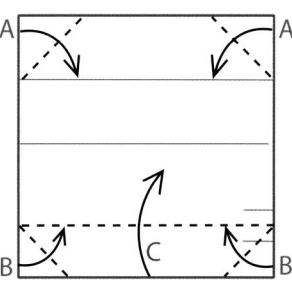

3. (A) Valley-fold the top corners to the nearest crease. (B) Valley-fold the bottom corners up to align with the nearest full crease. (C) Use the same crease to valley-fold the bottom edge up.

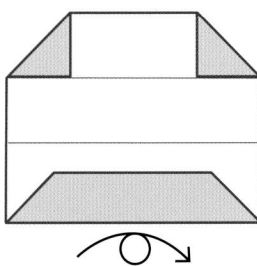

4. Turn the paper over, left to right.

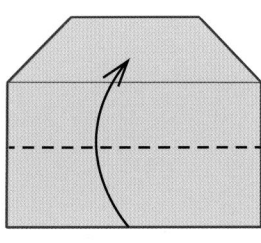

5. Use the lower crease to valley-fold the top edge up.

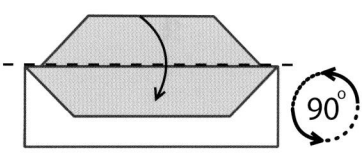

6. Valley-fold the top flap down and over the folded edge of the top layer. Rotate the paper 90 degrees counterclockwise.

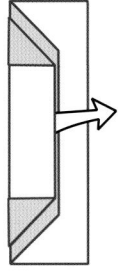

7. Open the paper.

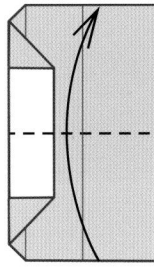

8. Valley-fold the bottom edge to the top.

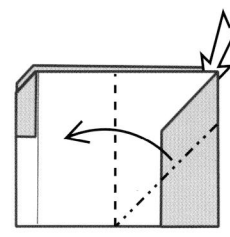

9. Squash-fold the right half.

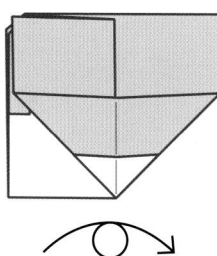

10. Your paper should look like this. Turn the paper over, left to right.

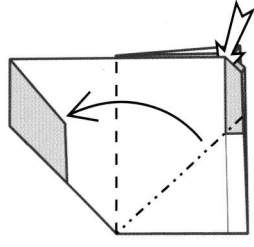

11. Squash-fold the right half.

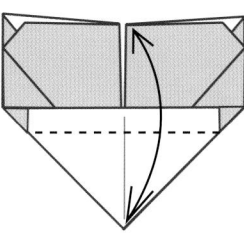

12. Valley-fold the bottom corner to the top of the split. Unfold.

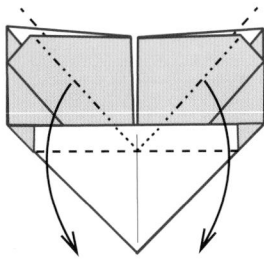

13. One at a time, squash-fold the upper right and left halves of the model, forming the wings.

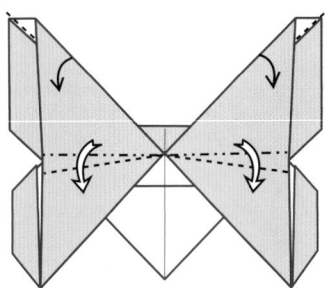

14. Move the top layer of the leading edge of the forewing down. Fold the mountain crease in the middle of the wing down, forming a wing overlap.

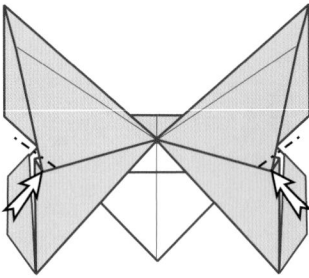

15. Inside-reverse fold the indicated corners.

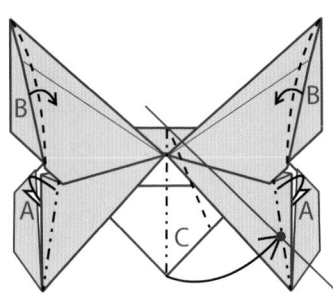

16. (A) Mountain-fold the indicated edges of the hindwings behind. (B) Valley-fold the raw edge of the forewing over, forming a lunule. (C) Mountain- and valley-fold the abdomen over the right wing.

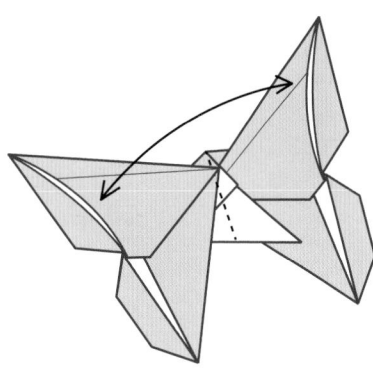

17. Valley-fold the left wing to match the right wing. Unfold.

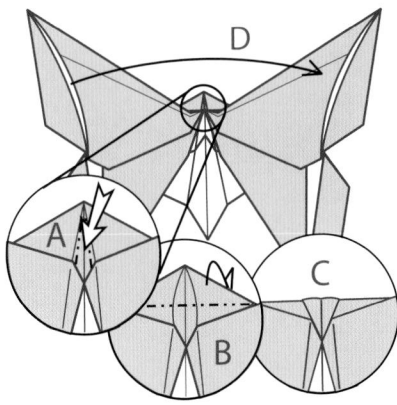

18. (A) Squash-fold the paper for the head. (B) Mountain-fold the corner behind. (C) Your paper should look like this. (D) Fold the wings together.

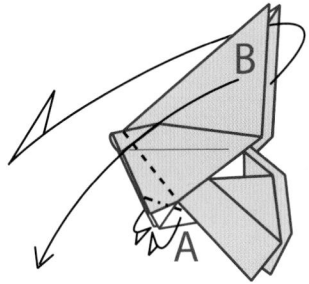

19. (A) Mountain-fold the abdomen edges inside. (B) Valley-fold the wings down on each side.

A Butterfly for Sok Song.

"A Butterfly for Sok" looks great with "Aztec" forewings. See if you can figure out how to fold this variation!

A Butterfly for Lillian Oppenheimer

"The Lillian"

The late Lillian Oppenheimer is often called our Grandmother of Origami in the U.S. Lillian's home was *the* gathering place. Her special magnetism attracted folders of all types.

"The Lillian" not only hosts others, she travels around, pollinating minds to learn and love origami.

can you come over?
I have a visiting guest
you simply must meet!

This design will introduce a different size margin on one end, resulting in the "Lillian Hindwing," as well as a different style for the forewing.

The *Automeris io* (Io) moth displays the eye-spots that serve as the real world inspiration for this model.

Photo by Patrick Coin. (Source: *http://upload.wikimedia.org/wikipedia/commons/c/cf/Automeris_ioFMPC-CA20040704-2974B1.jpg*)

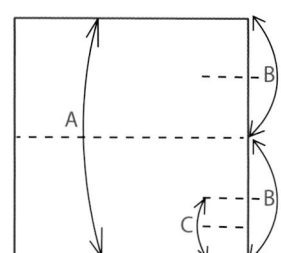

1. Begin with the minor color facing up. (A) Valley-fold in half, bottom edge to top. Unfold. (B) Valley-fold the top and the bottom edges to the center crease and make a pinch mark for each. Unfold. (C) Move the bottom edge to the lower crease line and make a pinch mark. Unfold.

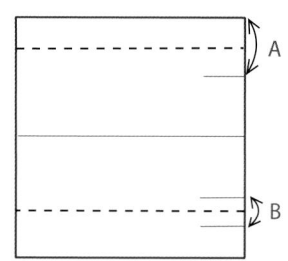

2. (A) Valley-fold the top edge of the paper to the top pinch mark. Unfold. (B) Lay the bottom pinch mark on top of the pinch mark above it and valley-fold all the way across the paper. Unfold.

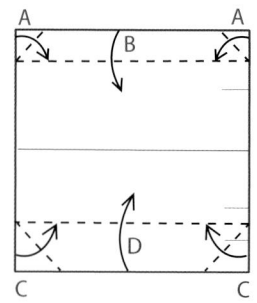

3. (A) Valley-fold the top corners to the nearest crease. (B) Use the same crease to valley-fold the top edge down. (C) Valley-fold the bottom corners up to align with the nearest full crease. (D) Use the same crease to valley-fold the bottom edge up.

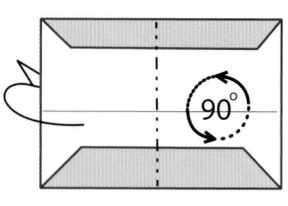

4. Mountain-fold the paper in half and rotate it 90 degrees counterclockwise.

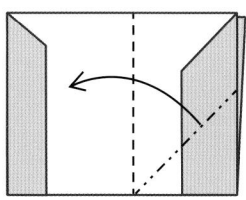

5. Squash-fold the right half.

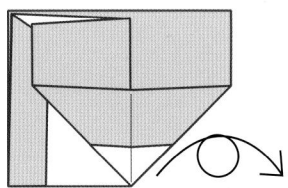

6. Your paper should look like this. Turn it over, left to right.

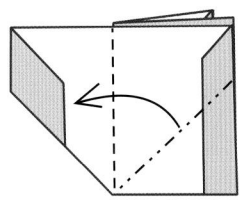

7. Squash-fold the right half.

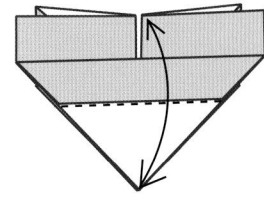

8. Valley-fold the bottom corner to the top of the split. Unfold.

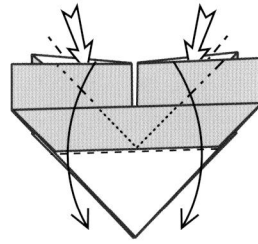

9. One at a time, squash-fold the upper right and left halves of the model, forming the wings.

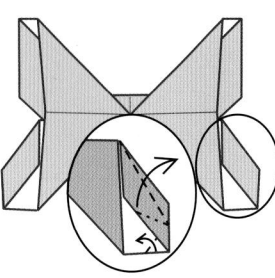

10. For both hindwings, valley-fold the top half of the layer of the hindwing out and form a squash fold on the bottom half.

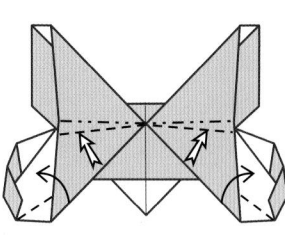

11. Move the top layer of the trailing edges of the hindwings up. Fold the mountain crease in the middle of the wing down, forming a wing overlap.

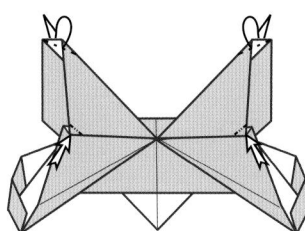

12. Mountain-fold the top edges of the forewings behind. Inside-reverse fold the indicated corners.

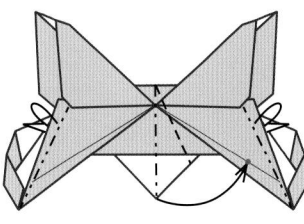

13. Mountain-fold the indicated edges of the hindwings behind. Mountain- and valley-fold the abdomen over the right wing.

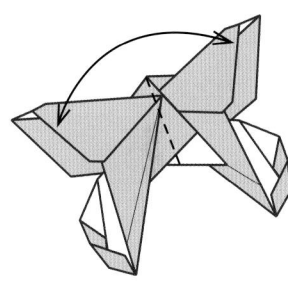

14. Valley-fold the left wing to match the right wing. Unfold.

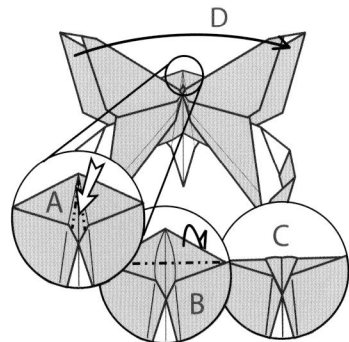

15. (A) Squash-fold the paper for the head. (B) Mountain-fold the corner behind. (C) Your paper should look like this. (D) Fold the wings together.

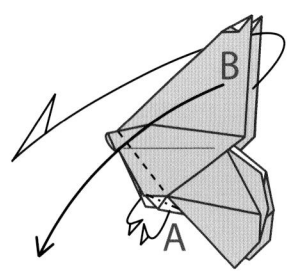

16. (A) Mountain-fold the abdomen edges inside. (B) Valley-fold the wings down on each side.

A Butterfly for Lillian Oppenheimer.

A Butterfly for Guy Kawasaki

"The Kawasaki Swallowtail"

This version was designed for entrepreneurial guru, Guy Kawasaki, to grace the cover of his tenth book, *Enchantment*. A Hawaiian of Japanese heritage, Guy's work embodies metamorphosis, unexpected delight, and the pollination-like spread of great ideas and winning attitudes. A variation of the popular Alexander Swallowtail, this design was originally folded in a composite of fine Japanese printed *washi*, and our handmade Origamido papers.

a competition
Enchantment's cover message:
folded swallowtail!

This design introduces both the "Swallowtail" hindwing, and the "Angelwing" treatment on the forewing.

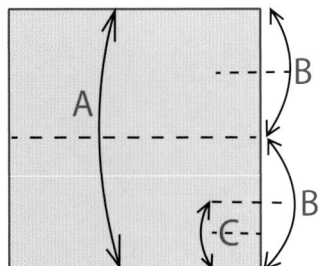

1. Begin with the major color facing up. (A) Valley-fold in half, bottom edge to top. Unfold. (B) Valley-fold the top and the bottom edges to the center crease and make a pinch mark for each. Unfold. (C) Move the bottom edge to the lower crease line and make a pinch mark. Unfold.

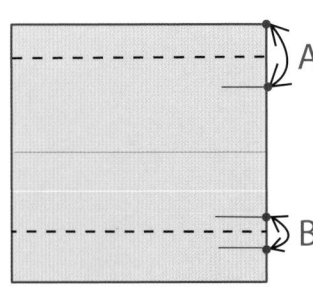

2. (A) Valley-fold the top edge of the paper to the top pinch mark. Unfold. (B) Lay the bottom pinch mark on top of the pinch mark above it and valley-fold all the way across the paper. Unfold.

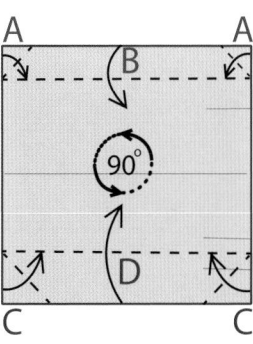

3. (A) Valley-fold the top corners to the nearest crease. (B) Use the same crease to valley-fold the top edge down. (C) Valley-fold the bottom corners up to align with the nearest full crease. (D) Use the same crease to valley-fold the bottom edge up. Rotate the paper 90 degrees counterclockwise.

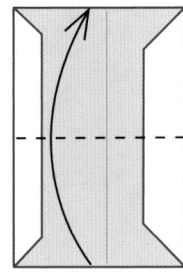

4. Valley-fold the paper in half, bottom to top.

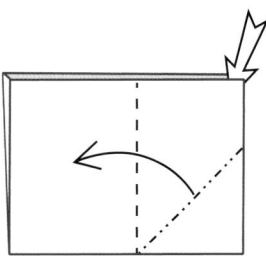

5. Squash-fold the right half.

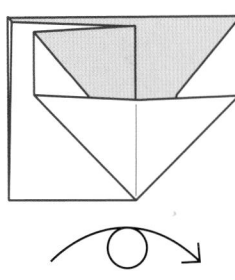

6. Your paper should look like this. Turn over, left to right.

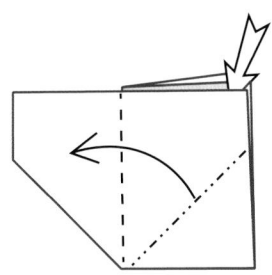

7. Squash-fold the right half.

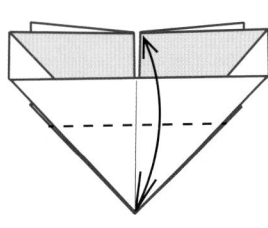

8. Valley-fold the bottom corner to the top of the split. Unfold.

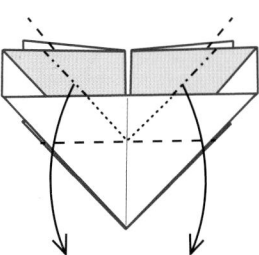

9. One at a time, squash-fold the upper right and left halves of the model, forming the wings.

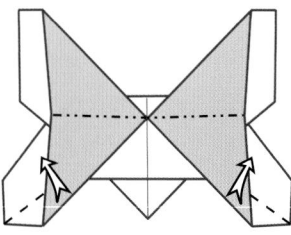

10. Move the top layer of the hindwings up, valley-folding the lower layers to the corners. Sharpen the middle mountain creases.

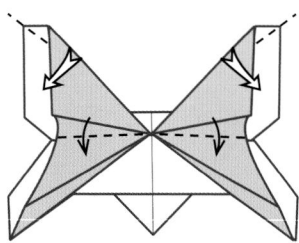

11. Move the top layer of the leading edge of each forewing down. Fold the mountain crease in the middle of each wing down, forming wing overlaps.

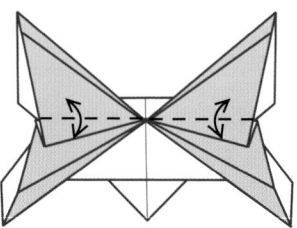

12. Valley-fold the folded edges up and then down. Apply the sequence that follows (steps 13–20) to each wing.

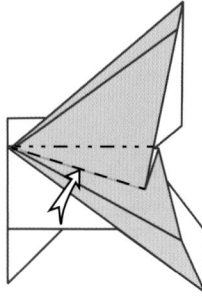

13. Inside-reverse fold.

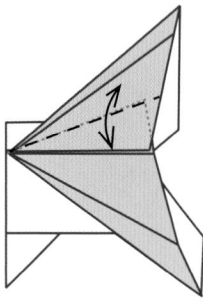

14. Valley-fold the folded edge to the crease above. Unfold.

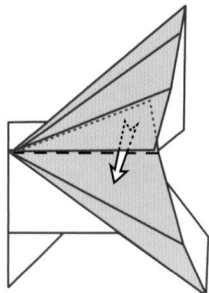

15. Pull out the hidden layer.

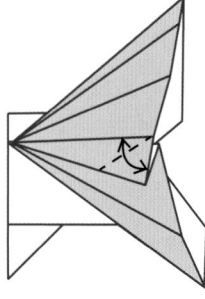

16. Precrease: valley-fold the short edge of the corner to the crease above. Unfold.

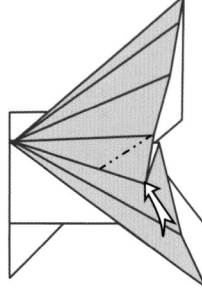

17. Inside-reverse fold the precreased corner.

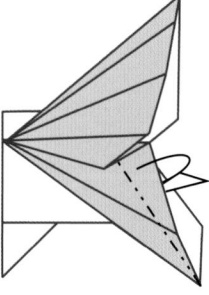

18. Mountain-fold the indicated edge behind.

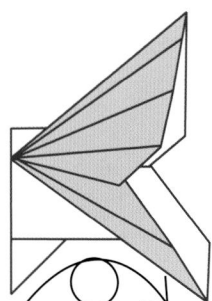

19. Turn the paper over, left to right.

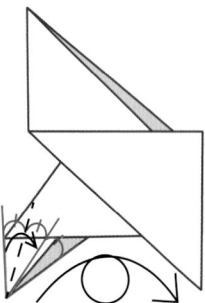

20. Valley-fold the outside edge one-third over. Turn the paper over, left to right.

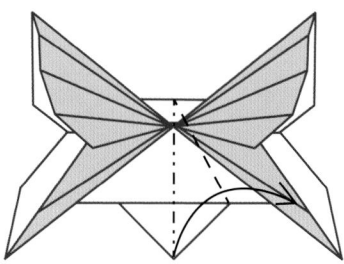

21. Mountain- and valley-fold the abdomen over the right wing.

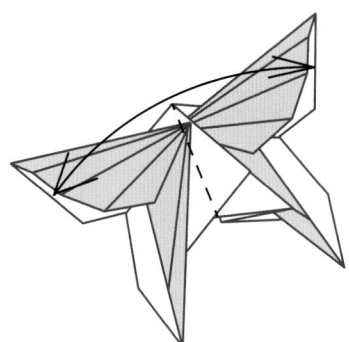

22. Valley-fold the left wing to match the right wing. Unfold.

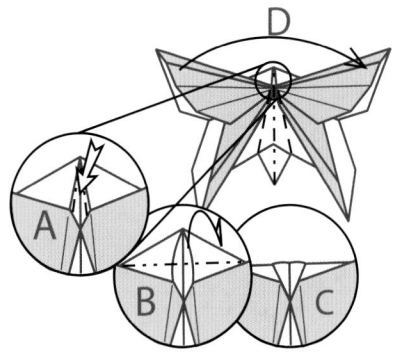

23. (A) Squash-fold the paper for the head. (B) Mountain-fold the corner behind. (C) Your paper should look like this. (D) Fold the wings together.

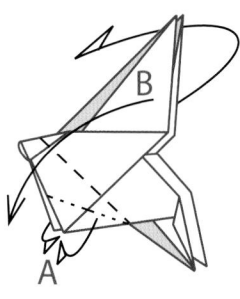

24. (A) Mountain-fold the abdomen edges inside. (B) Valley-fold the wings down on each side.

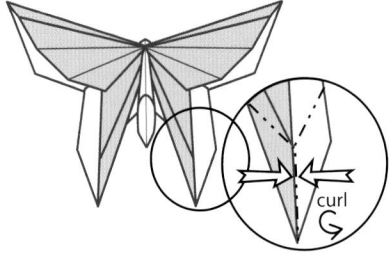

25. Mountain-fold the bottom corner of the hindwings in half. Gently curve them outward.

A Butterfly for Guy Kawasaki.

The Origamido Butterfly

This special design is named for the Origamido Studio. "The Origamido Butterfly" has segmented wings, clean lines, and a color-change body. The distinctive shape made this design a clear choice for our Origamido Studio logo, because it was elegant, confident, finished, and free—so different from traditional attempts at origami butterflies, which often seemed unfinished or even tortured.

Origamido!
paper folding is the craft
"do," a life's journey!

This design introduces the "Origamido Butterfly Base," and a different style of finishing the butterfly's head.

The *Morpho didius* (Giant Blue Morpho) butterfly was the real world inspiration for this model.

Photo by Didier Descouens. (Source: *http://upload.wikimedia.org/wikipedia/commons/e/ee/Morpho_didius_Male_Dos_MHNT.jpg*)

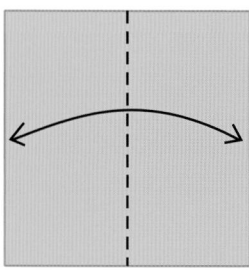

1. Begin with the major color facing up. Valley-fold the paper in half, edge to edge. Unfold.

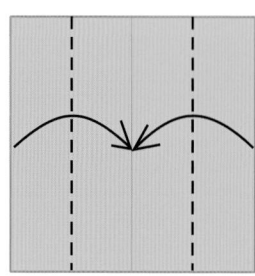

2. Valley-fold two opposite edges to meet at the crease.

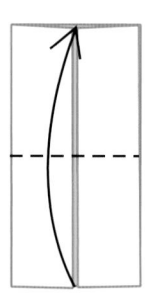

3. Valley-fold the paper in half, bottom edge to top.

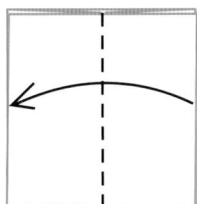

4. Valley-fold the paper in half, right to left.

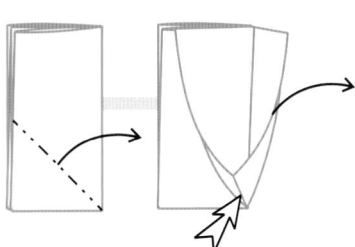

5. Open the top half and squash-fold.

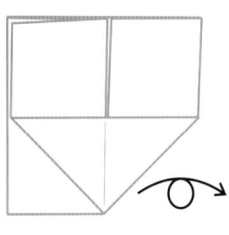

6. Your paper should look like this. Turn it over, left to right.

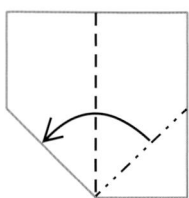

7. Squash-fold the right half.

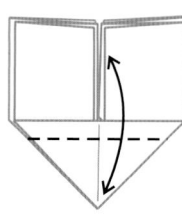

8. Valley-fold the bottom corner up. Make the fold below the top edge of the triangle area at approximately one-fifth the height of the triangle. Unfold.

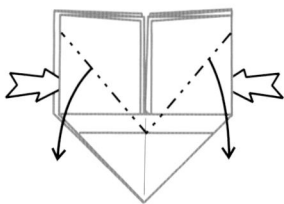

9. One at a time, squash-fold the upper left and right halves to form the wings.

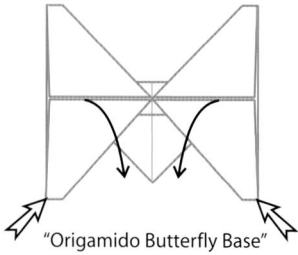

"Origamido Butterfly Base"

10. This is the "Origamido Butterfly Base." Countless design variations are possible from here! Open the two bottom flaps and squash-fold the bottom left and right corners.

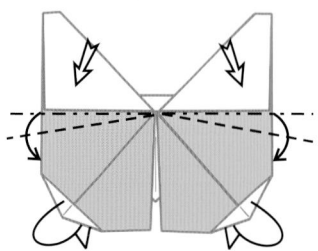

11. *Carefully* turn the triangle pockets of the hindwings inside out, moving them to the backside. Move the leading edges of the forewings down and crimp the middle of the wings, forming the overlap.

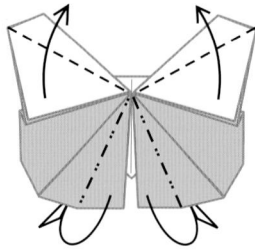

12. Valley-fold the folded edges up and then down.

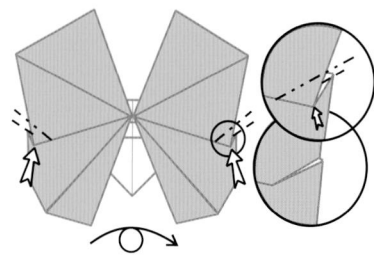

13. Inside-reverse fold the indicated corners. Turn the model over, left to right.

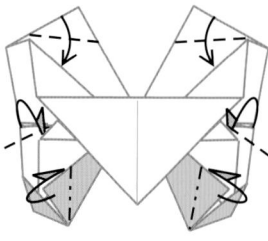

14. Mountain-fold the corner flaps of the hindwings. Valley-fold the top edge of each forewing to its nearby, folded edge. Valley-fold the middle corners over and tuck behind the folded layer.

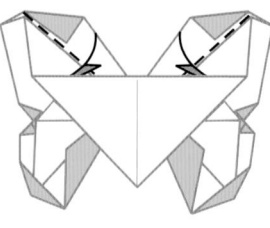

15. Valley-fold the top edges down and tuck behind the top edge of the triangle layer.

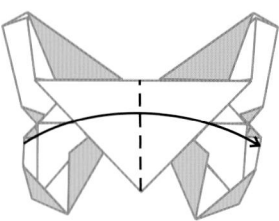

16. Valley-fold the model in half, wing to wing.

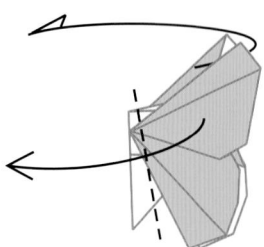

17. Valley-fold each wing over the body. Notice the angle of the fold line.

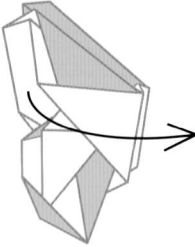

18. Open the wings out to each side of the body.

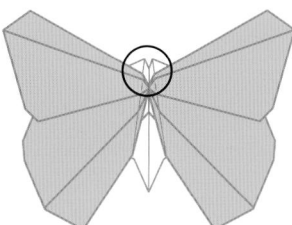

19. Detail follows: Forming the Origamido Butterfly Head.

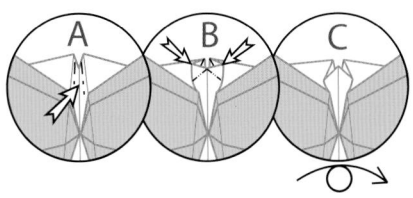

20. (A) Squash-fold the paper for the head. (B) Inside-reverse-fold the indicated corners. (C) Turn the model over, left to right.

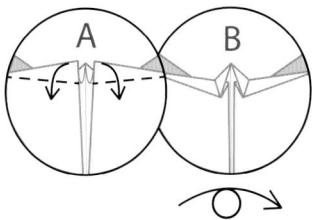

21. (A) Valley-fold the top edges down. (B) Turn the model over, left to right.

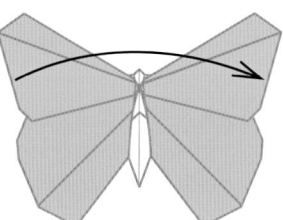

22. Valley-fold the wings together.

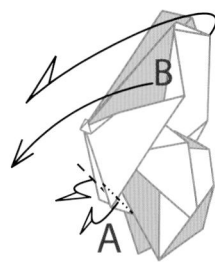

23. (A) Mountain-fold the abdomen edges in. (B) Open the wings.

The Origamido Butterfly.

Origamido Butterfly variation: Omit turning the triangle pockets inside out at step 11.

The Boston Butterfly

Thanks to the QVC home shopping cable network, we introduced this variation of the Origamido Butterfly on the first video mass-market origami kit!

Boston pioneers
valuable tea tossed over
what have we started?

This design introduces a color-change between forewings and hindwings, and it can be attractive when folded with or without eyespots.

The *Colias hyale* (Pale Clouded Yellow) butterfly was the real world inspiration for this model.

Photo by Dumi. (Source: *http://upload. wikimedia.org/wikipedia/commons/d/d1/ Colias_hyale.male.jpg*)

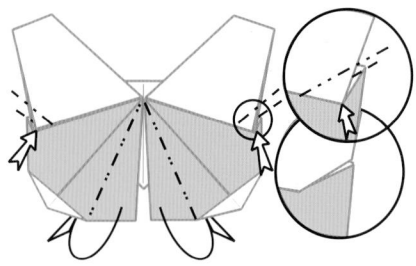

Fold through step 11 of the Origamido Butterfly (page 82). Mountain-fold the inner edges of the hindwings behind. Inside-reverse-fold the indicated corners.

The Boston Butterfly.

The Question Mark

This popular variation of the Origamido Butterfly plays with the marginal edges of the wing, making them fancy and full of curves.

everyone wonders
fancy edges on margins...
can Question Marks fly?

This design introduces dimpled hindwing edges.

The *Polygonia interrogationis* (Question Mark) butterfly displays wing scalloping that serves as the real world inspiration for this model.

Photo by Michael A. Kelly. (Source: *http://www. fws.gov/morganbrake/images/BUTTERFLYques- tion.jpg*)

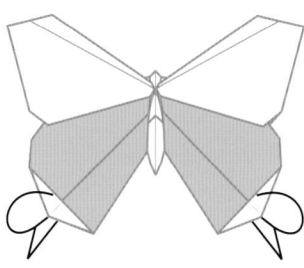

1. Fold the Boston Butterfly (opposite). *Carefully* turn the triangle pockets inside out.

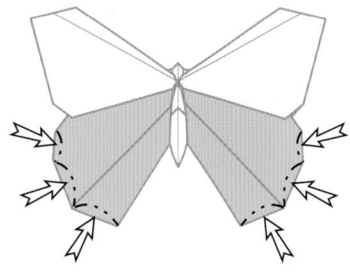

2. Install a curving mountain fold at each flat edge of the hindwings.

The Question Mark.

A Butterfly for Doris Asano

"The Doris"

This design is named for Doris Asano, the chief organizer of avid Arizona paper folders. She is the person responsible for bringing us to Phoenix for advanced paper folding workshops. The first visit lead to our big origami art exhibition at the Arizona-Sonora Desert Museum in Tucson, and 50,000 fans!

"The Doris" butterfly loves to laugh in the sunshine. She enjoys visiting all of her desert friends, and gets excited when rare rains make the desert burst into bloom. "The Doris" takes good care of visiting butterflies from near and far. All are welcome and are immediately drawn into her laughter and friendship.

> *friendship is like air*
> *without friends, we can't exist*
> *breathe deeply today*

This design will introduce a different forewing shape.

The *Danaus plexippus* (Monarch) butterfly was the real world inspiration for this model.

Photo by Kenneth Dwain Harrelson. (Source: *http://upload.wikimedia.org/wikipedia/commons/6/63/Monarch_In_May.jpg*)

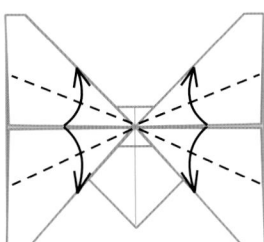

"Origamido Butterfly Base"

1. Fold up to the "Origamido Butterfly Base" (step 10) of the Origamido Butterfly project (page 82). Valley-fold the raw edges of the top layers out and align each to its adjacent folded edge.

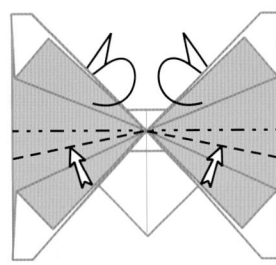

2. Turn the top layers of the forewings inside out, and to the back. Move the top layers of the hindwings upward and crimp the middle area of each wing.

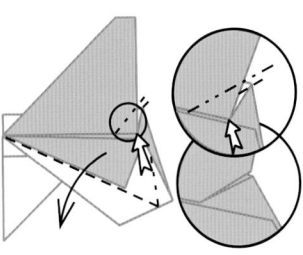

3. Inside-reverse fold the indicated corner. Move the top layer of the hindwing down and squash-fold the outer corner.

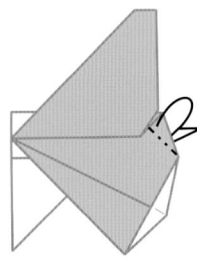

4. Mountain-fold the indicated corner behind.

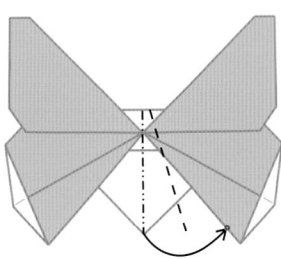

5. Mountain- and valley-fold the abdomen over the right wing.

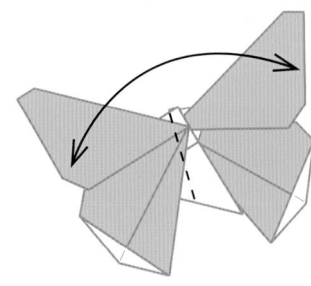

6. Valley-fold the wings to match. Open the wings out to each side of the body.

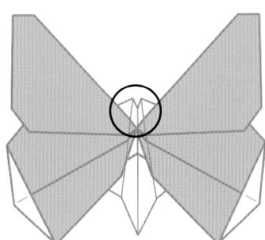

7. Detail follows: Forming the Origamido Butterfly Head.

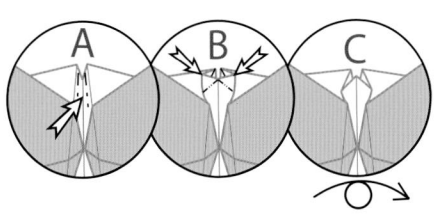

8. (A) Squash-fold the paper for the head. (B) Inside-reverse-fold the indicated corners. (C) Turn the model over.

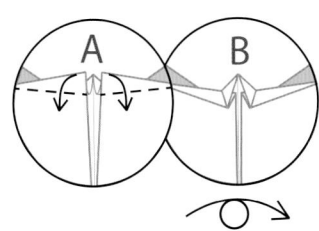

9. (A) Valley-fold the top edges down. (B) Turn the model over.

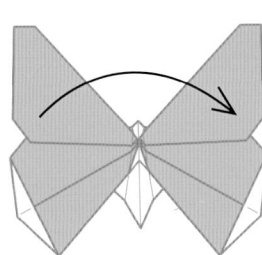

10. Valley-fold the wings together.

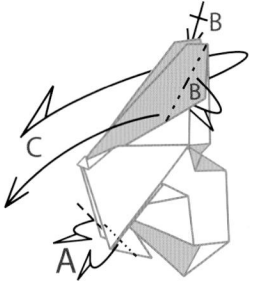

11. (A) Mountain-fold the abdomen edges in. (B) Mountain-fold the indicated edges behind. (C) Open the wings.

A Butterfly for Doris Asano.

A Butterfly for Diana Wolf

"The Diana"

"The Diana" was named for our inspirational poet and folding friend from Arizona. Diana Wolf, Doris Asano, and a small handful of others maintain a robust folding group in the Phoenix area. Check out the Heritage Square Matsuri in Phoenix.

> *deep inside her heart*
> *a folded she-wolf sings out*
> *howl to raise the moon!*

This design will introduce an asymmetrical squash-fold to produce a color change on the wings.

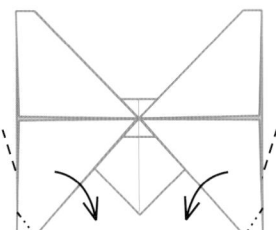

"Origamido Butterfly Base"

1. Fold up to the "Origamido Butterfly Base" (step 10) of the Origamido Butterfly project (page 82). Open the top layers of the hindwings and squash-fold the outer corners, forming asymmetrical, triangular pockets that are taller at the top and wider at the bottom.

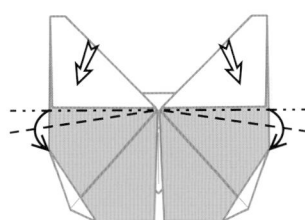

2. Move the top layers of the forewings downward and crimp the middle area of each wing.

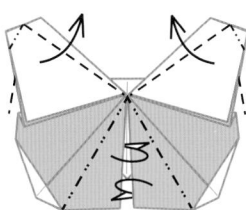

3. Mountain-fold the raw edges of the hindwings to the back. Valley-fold the top layers of the forewings up and squash-fold triangular pockets, similar in shape to those on the hindwings.

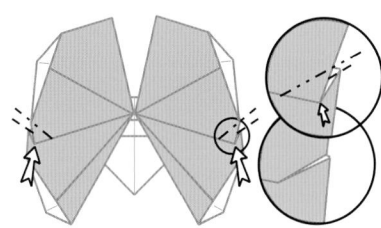

4. Inside-reverse-fold the indicated corners.

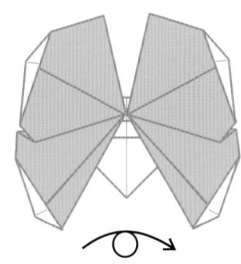

5. Turn the model over, left to right.

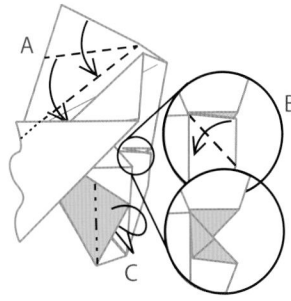

6. (A) Valley-fold the top edges of the forewings down to the crease. Valley-fold the resulting flap down and behind the top edge of the large triangle. (B) Valley-fold the middle corner down. (C) Mountain-fold the corner flap of each hindwing behind.

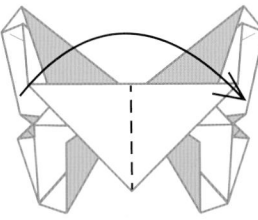

7. Valley-fold the model in half, wing to wing.

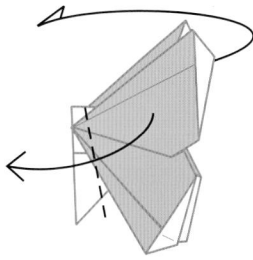

8. Valley-fold each wing over and against the body. Notice the angle of the fold line.

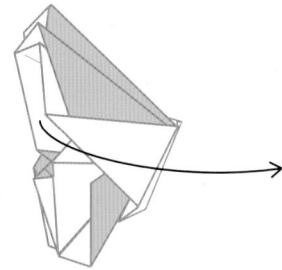

9. Open the wings out to each side of the body.

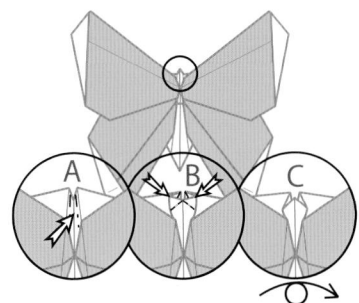

10. (A) Squash-fold the paper for the head. (B) Inside-reverse-fold the indicated corners. (C) Turn over the model over, left to right.

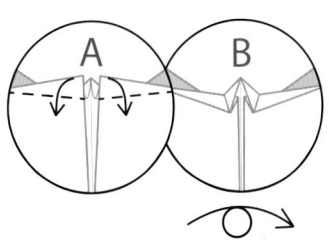

11. (A) Valley-fold the top edges down. (B) Turn the model over, left to right. Open the wings.

A Butterfly for Diana Wolf.

A Butterfly for V'Ann Cornelius

"The V'Ann"

Named for the late V'Ann Cornelius, folder and origami art curator responsible for art exhibitions at numerous origami conventions, and at the Mingei Museum in San Diego, California; Hangar Ten in Salzburg, Austria; and for several other shows and exhibits.

"The V'Ann" loves to put on a show. She will direct the talent, and expertly determine what goes where, how, and when. Her x-ray vision sees inner beauty, besides knowing which is the best side to display. She makes sure the exhibits are spotless, adjusts the lights, raises the pedestal, and places the freshest flowers at either side.

send me the best work
raise it to the high platform
come, look at it now!

This design will introduce color-change flaps for the top paper.

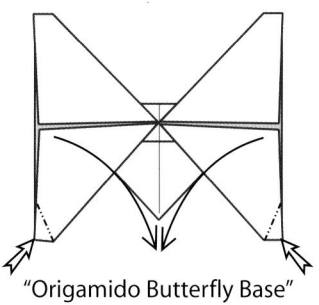

"Origamido Butterfly Base"

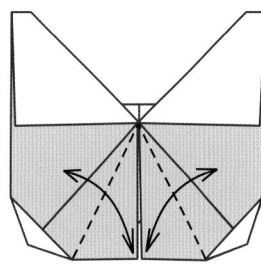

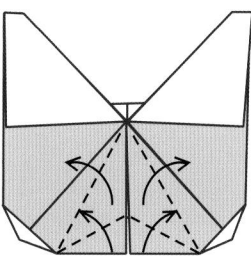

1. Fold up to the "Origamido Butterfly Base" (step 10) of the Origamido Butterfly project (page 82). Open the top layers of the hindwings and squash-fold the outer corners, forming triangular pockets.

2. Valley-fold and unfold the raw edges of the hindwings, making a crease that spans from the interior center of each wing down to the bottom corners of the triangle pockets.

3. Valley-fold the bottom edges of the hindwings to the crease, and then valley-fold the resulting flap over, on top of each hindwing.

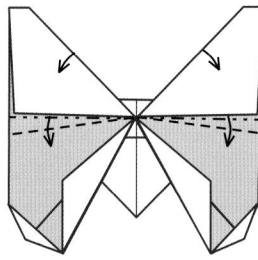

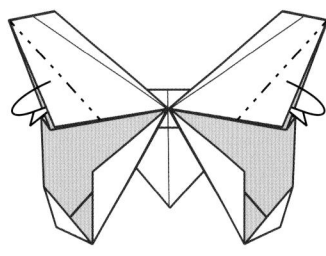

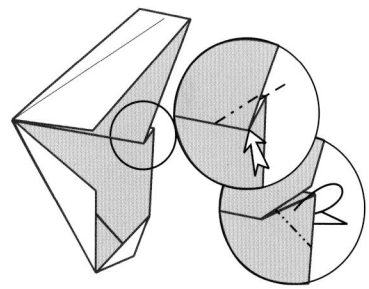

4. Move the leading edges of the forewings down and crimp the middle of the wings, forming the overlap.

5. Mountain-fold the raw edge of top layer of each forewing behind.

6. Inside-reverse-fold the indicated corners. Mountain-fold the free corner behind.

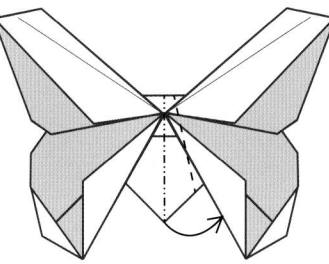

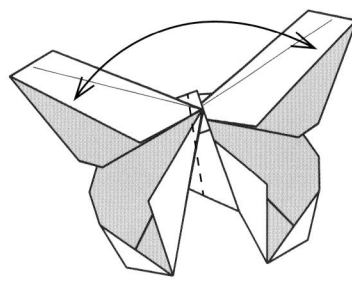

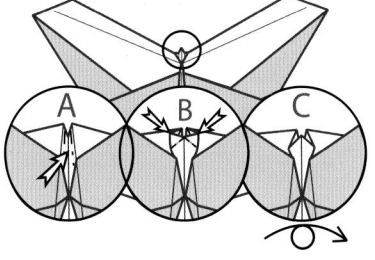

7. Mountain- and valley-fold the abdomen over the right wing. Notice the angle of the fold line.

8. Valley-fold the wings to match. Open the wings out to each side of the body.

9. (A) Squash-fold the paper for the head. (B) Inside-reverse-fold the indicated corners. (C) Turn the model over, left to right.

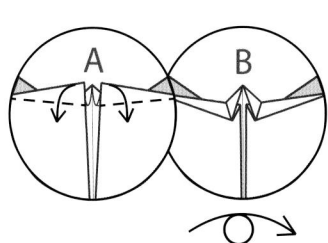

10. (A) Valley-fold the top edges down. (B) Turn the model over, left to right. Open the wings.

A Butterfly for V'Ann Cornelius.

A Butterfly for June Sakamoto

"The June"

This beautiful butterfly is named for our longtime friend, and tireless volunteer and organizer for Origami USA, and now co-owner of the Mountain-Valley Paper Company in South San Francisco, California.

Through June, we are reminded of the complex, mysterious richness of Japan. Despite strong forces of time and circumstance, her embodiment of the subtle strength of Japan keeps reminding us about a different way, a better way. While so many people just watch, June will put on the Kimono and make sure that the job gets done right.

> *prepare for all things*
> *and help whenever able*
> *oh my! They're here now?*

This design will introduce folding the square in thirds, as well as finishing the hindwings with lovely fanfolds.

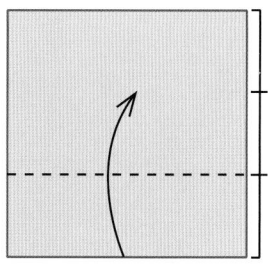

1. Begin with the minor color facing up. Valley-fold the bottom third of the square up.

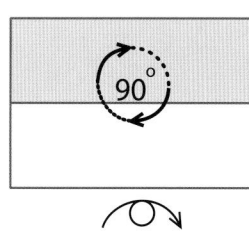

2. Your paper should look like this. Rotate the paper 90 degrees clockwise and turn it over.

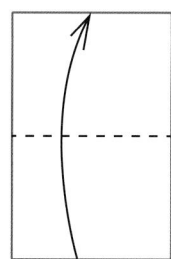

3. Valley-fold the paper in half, bottom edge to top.

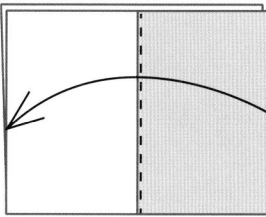

4. Valley-fold the paper in half, right to left.

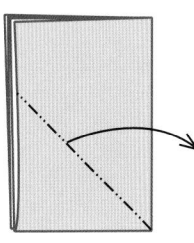

5. Squash-fold the top half of the paper.

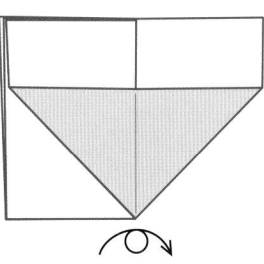

6. Your paper should look like this. Turn it over, left to right.

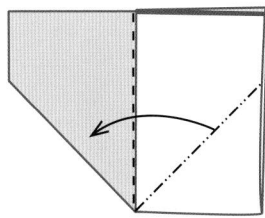

7. Squash-fold the right half of the paper.

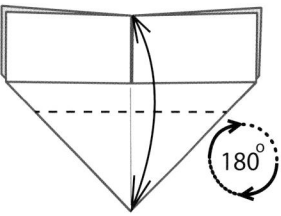

8. Valley-fold the bottom corner to the top of the split. Unfold. Rotate the paper 180 degrees.

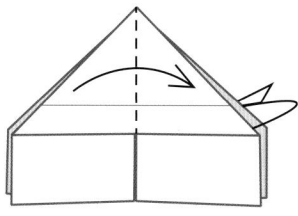

9. Rearrange the flaps: left to right, in front, and right to left, behind.

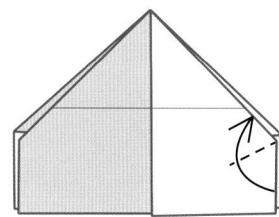

10. Your paper should look like this. Align the short, vertical right edge with the folded edge above. Make a pinch mark.

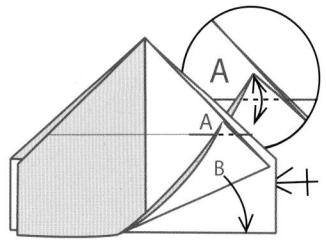

11. (A) Valley-fold the flap's corner down at the level of the horizontal crease. (B) Return flap to the bottom. Repeat behind.

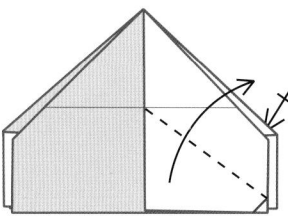

12. Valley-fold between the indicated points, squash-folding at the bottom corner. Repeat behind.

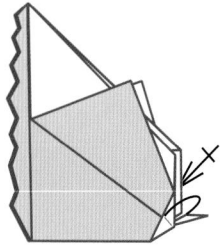

13. Carefully turn the triangle pocket inside out. Repeat behind.

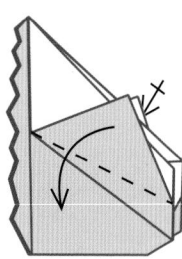

14. Valley-fold the top flap down. Repeat behind.

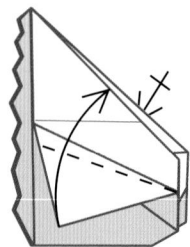

15. Valley-fold the flap up, making the corner touch the folded edge above. Repeat behind.

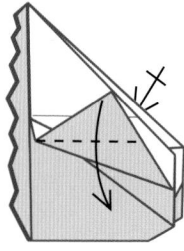

16. Valley-fold the flap down, making a folded edge that is parallel to the horizontal crease above. Repeat behind.

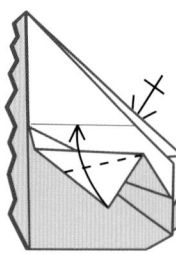

17. Valley-fold the flap up, making the corner touch the horizontal crease above. Repeat behind.

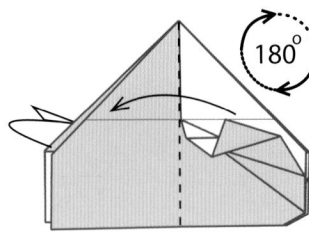

18. Rearrange the flaps: right to left in front, and left to right behind. Rotate the paper 180 degrees.

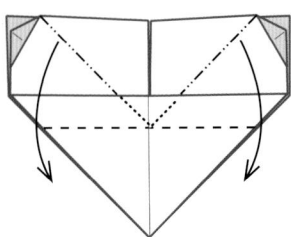

19. One at a time, squash-fold the upper left and right halves of the paper to form the wings.

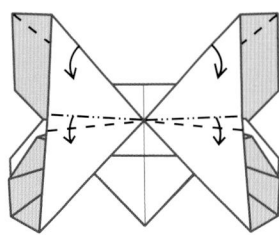

20. Move the top layers of the forewings downward and crimp the middle area of each wing.

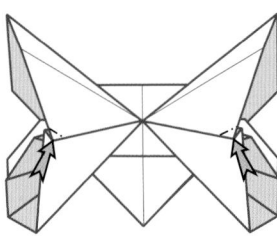

21. Inside-reverse-fold the indicated corners.

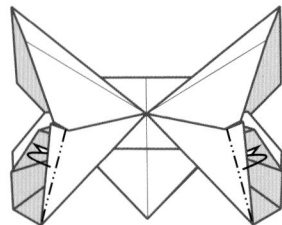

22. Mountain-fold the raw edges of the hindwings behind.

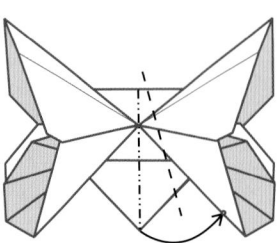

23. Mountain- and valley-fold the abdomen over the right wing. Notice the angle of the fold line.

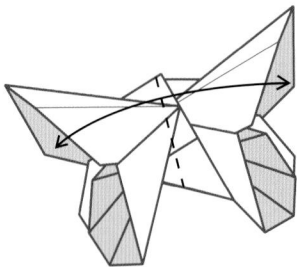

24. Valley-fold the wings to match. Open the wings out to each side of the body.

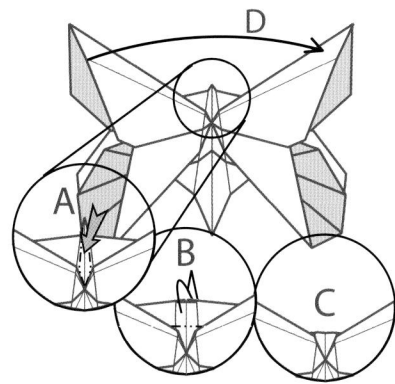

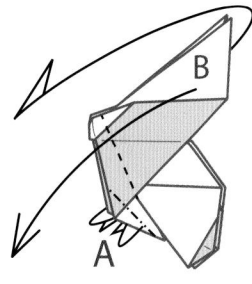

25. (A) Squash-fold the paper for the head. (B) Mountain-fold the corner behind. (C) Your paper should look like this. (D) Fold the wings together.

26. (A) Mountain-fold the abdomen edges inside. (B) Valley-fold the wings down on each side.

A Butterfly for June Sakamoto.

A Butterfly for Anne LaVin

"The Anne"

This design is named for Anne LaVin, origami creator, teacher, cyber-world master of origami websites and our new digital realities.

"The Anne" is our keeper of the cyber-keys, as comfortable in the computer ether as she is in the sheet-forming vat technologies of two thousand years ago. "The Anne" is at ease in the MIT or New York City classroom as she is on the high seas.

> *sails ships on high seas*
> *bytes and chips, learns Japanese*
> *all this, for pond weed!*

This design will introduce an inside-reverse swivel for a distinctive, geometric look. As diagramed, the model displays the hindwing configuration of my original gift to Anne. On the DVD, I demonstrate a version with the hindwing pockets turned inside out, a popular and elegant variation.

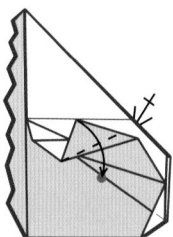

1. Fold up through step 17 (omitting step 13—don't turn the triangle pocket inside-out) of A Butterfly for June Sakamoto (page 94). Valley-fold the top flap down, making the corner touch the indicated folded edge.

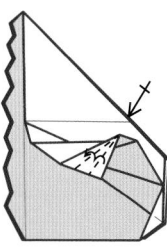

2. Narrow the flap by valley-folding the paper over and over, in thirds.

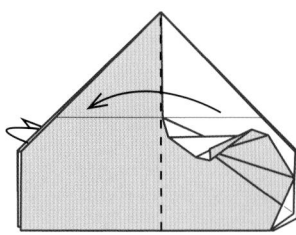

3. Rearrange the flaps: left to right, in front, and right to left, behind. Rotate the paper 180 degrees.

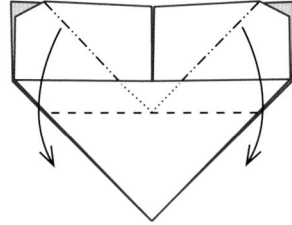

4. One at a time, squash-fold the upper left and right halves of the paper to form the wings. Look ahead to see the shape.

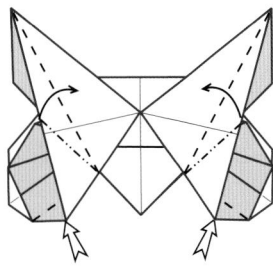

5. Move the top layers of the wings inward while moving the trailing edges upward. Squash-fold to flatten. Look ahead for the shape.

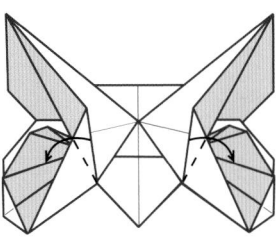

6. Valley-fold each flap over.

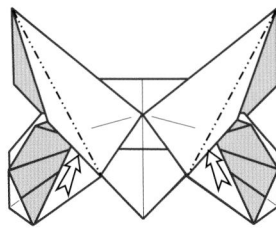

7. Inside-reverse fold the indicated flap on each wing.

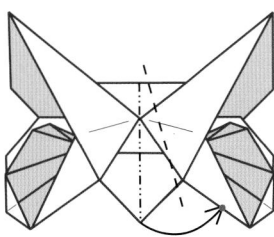

8. Mountain- and valley-fold the abdomen over the right wing. Notice the angle of the fold line.

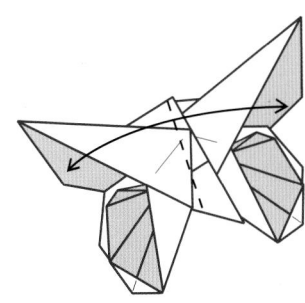

9. Valley-fold the wings to match. Open the wings out to each side of the body.

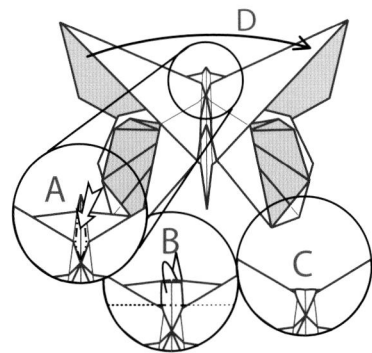

10. (A) Squash-fold the paper for the head. (B) Mountain-fold the corner behind. (C) Your paper should look like this. (D) Fold the wings together.

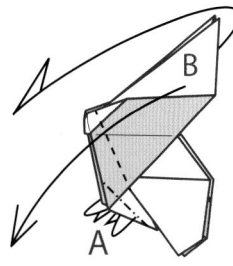

11. (A) Mountain-fold the abdomen edges inside. (B) Valley-fold the wings down on each side.

A Butterfly for Anne LaVin.

A Butterfly for Kyoto

Just before this book was printed, I was inspired by a pending trip to Kyoto, Japan. I designed this new butterfly with the city's history of the Japanese folding fan, and the lovely Yuzen fabric and papers, for which they are famous.

shimmering city
fragrant home of the geisha
forever beckons

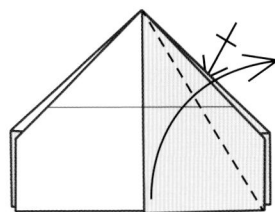

1. Fold up to step 10 for "A Butterfly for June Sakamoto" (page 94). Valley-fold the trapezoid flap out as far as possible. Repeat behind.

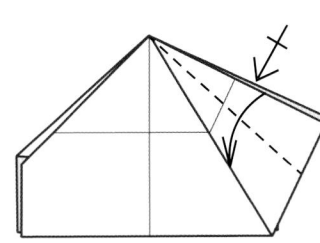

2. Valley-fold the triangle flap in half. Repeat behind.

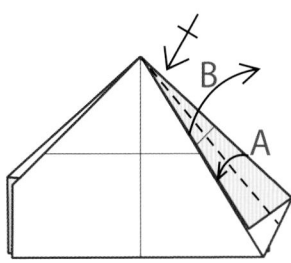

3. (A) Valley-fold the triangle flap in half. (B) Unfold the triangle flap completely. Repeat behind.

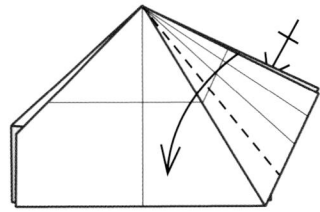

4. Valley-fold the triangle flap using the lower third crease. Repeat behind.

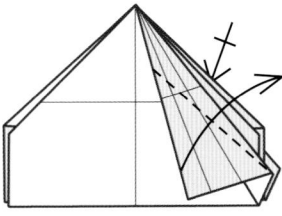

5. Valley-fold the square corner of the triangle flap out so that the uppermost edge becomes perpendicular to the vertical center crease. Repeat behind.

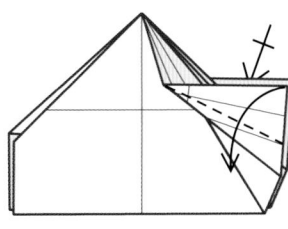

6. Valley-fold the triangle flap down, beginning at the end of the lower crease line. Repeat behind.

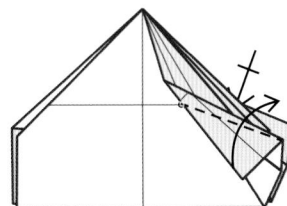

7. Valley-fold the triangle flap up so that the inside end of the fold starts at the level of the horizontal center crease. Repeat behind.

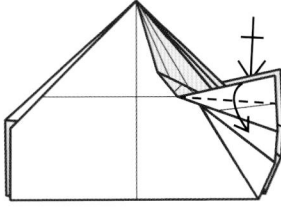

8. Valley-fold the triangle flap down, beginning at the end of the final crease line. Repeat behind.

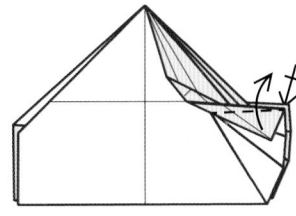

9. Valley-fold the triangle flap up. Repeat behind.

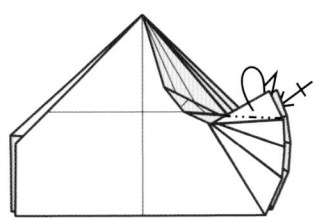

10. Mountain-fold the excess behind the top edge of the hindwing. Repeat behind.

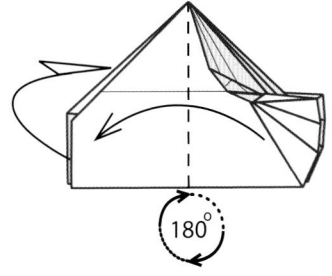

11. Fold the top right layer to the left and the back left layer to the right. Rotate the model 180 degrees.

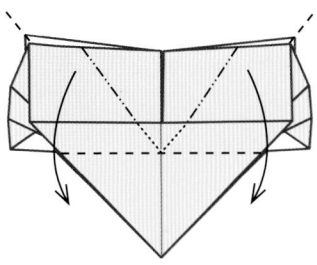

12. Squash-fold the hindwings down.

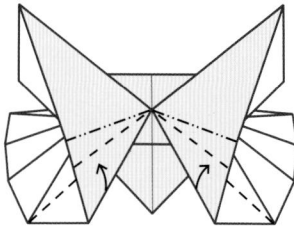

13. Make the wing overlaps by mountain-folding the existing horizontal wing creases and valley-folding crimps underneath. Take up paper from the trailing edges of the hindwings, folding to the limit of the outer bottom corners.

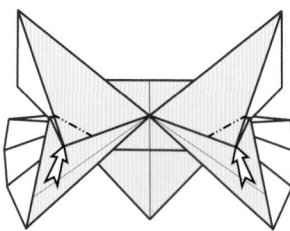

14. Inside-reverse-fold the indicated corners.

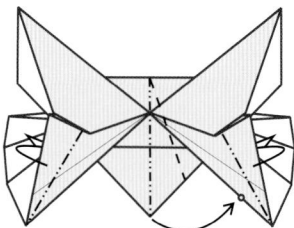

15. Mountain-fold the excess edges of the hindwings inside. Mountain-fold the vertical center crease of the body paper and swivel to make the bottom corner meet the back edge of the wing.

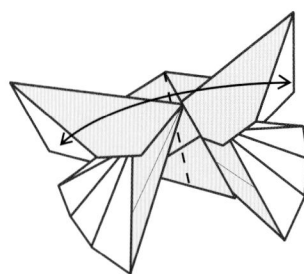

16. Valley-fold, wing to wing, and unfold.

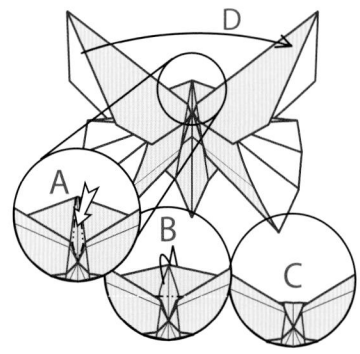

17. (A) Squash-fold the head paper. (B) Mountain-fold behind. (C) The completed head. (D) Bring the wings together.

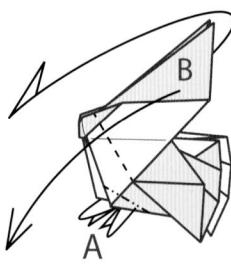

18. (A) Mountain-fold the corners in to taper the abdomen. (B) Open the wings out.

The completed female version of A Butterfly for Kyoto.

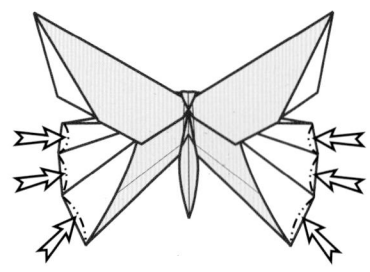

Variation: to make the male version of this butterfly, crescent-shaped mountain folds to scallop the facets of the hindwings.

The completed male version of A Butterfly for Kyoto.

A Butterfly for Russell Cashdollar

"The Cashdollar"

This design is a version of the "Joyce Rockmore" butterfly that we named for Russell Cashdollar, origami designer . "The Cashdollar" pays homage to Russell's colorful origami butterfly displays that we saw at the 1992 origami convention in New York City. It has fanciful color-change spots, and a proportion reminiscent of the design that Russell was exploring decades ago. His display inspired Michael to develop his own origami butterfly design system.

The *Dryas iulia* (Julia) butterfly displays the general wing shape that serves as the real world inspiration for this model.

Photo by Maurício Leonardi. (Source: *http://upload.wikimedia.org/wikipedia/commons/b/b4/Borboletajulia.jpg*)

> *paper folds grab me*
> *and take me on a journey!*
> *where will I go next?*

This design will introduce the "Longwing Base," also used to fold the "Butterfly for Joyce Rockmore" (featured in the *Origami Butterflies* kit, Tuttle Publishing, 2009) and related variations.

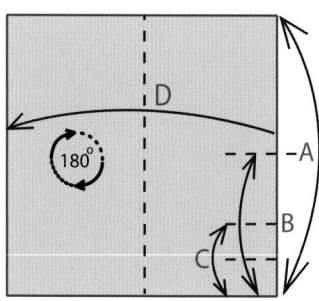

1. Begin with the major color facing up. (A) Bottom edge to top, make a pinch mark and unfold. (B) Bottom edge to pinch mark "A," make a new pinch and unfold. (C) Bottom edge to pinch mark "B," make a pinch mark and unfold. (D) Valley-fold in half, right to left, and then rotate 180 degrees.

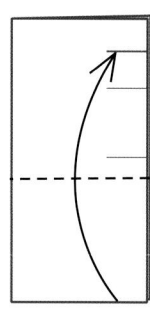

2. Valley-fold the bottom edge to the top pinch mark.

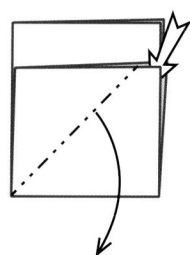

3. Squash-fold.

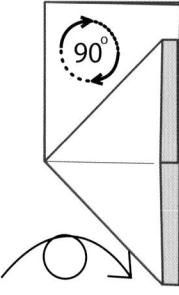

4. Your paper should look like this. Rotate 90 degrees clockwise. Turn over, left to right.

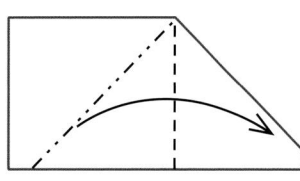

5. Squash-fold.

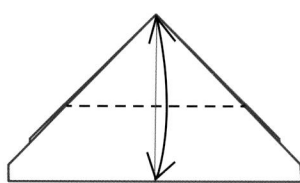

6. Valley-fold the top corner to the middle of the bottom edge. Unfold.

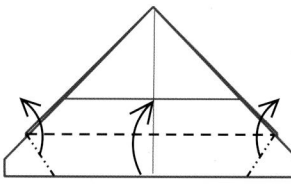

7. Valley-fold the bottom edge of the top layer up to the crease and then squash-fold the left and right pockets. Look ahead at the next step for the shape.

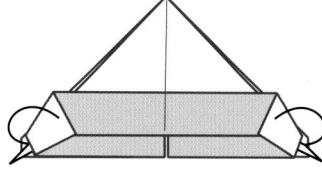

8. Turn the pockets inside out.

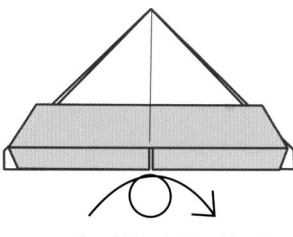

9. Your paper should look like this. Turn over, left to right.

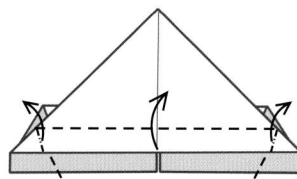

10. Valley-fold the bottom edge of the top layer up to the crease and then squash-fold the left and right pockets. Look ahead at the next step for the shape.

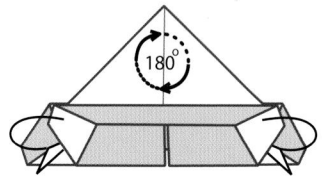

11. Turn the pockets inside out. Rotate 180 degrees.

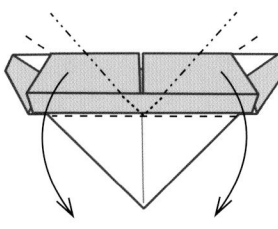

12. One at a time, squash-fold the right and left halves of the model to form the wings. Look ahead at the next step for the shape.

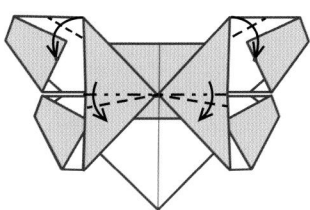

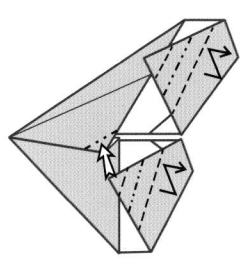

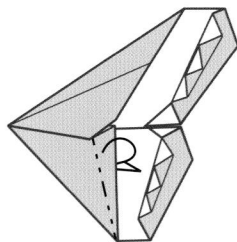

13. Form a crimped overlap at the middle of each wing by rolling the top edges and the bottom edges of each wing downward. Mountain and valley-fold the paper at the middle of each wing, creating the overlap.

14. Inside-reverse-fold the wing corners for both wings. Mountain- and valley-fold the forewing and hindwing flaps into thirds, forming a pattern of alternating colored triangles.

15. Mountain-fold the indicated flap on each wing.

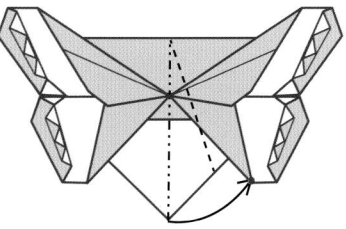

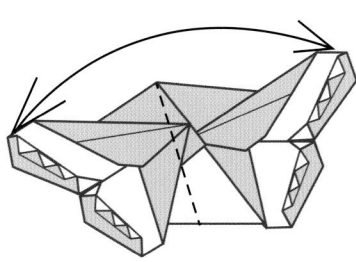

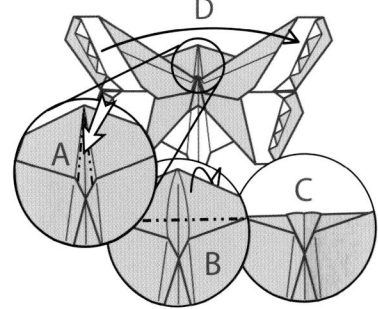

16. Mountain and valley-fold the abdomen over the right wing. Notice the angle of the fold line.

17. Valley-fold the wings to match. Open the wings out to each side of the body.

18. (A) Squash-fold the paper for the head. (B) Mountain-fold the corner behind. (C) Your paper should look like this. (D) Fold the wings together.

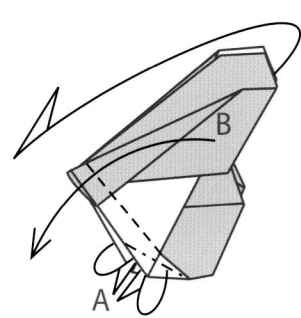

19. (A) Mountain-fold the abdomen edges inside. (B) Valley-fold the wings down on each side.

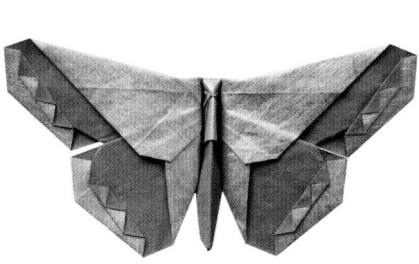

A Butterfly for Russell Cashdollar.

The Mudarri Luna Moth

This design is named for Greg Mudarri, who picked up a magazine and was instantly captivated by a haunting image on the cover: a human riding a paper crane! He sought out the Origamido Studio for folding lessons, and soon became our good friend and helped us with graphic art. Greg is also an origami creator and he taught many lessons at the Origamido Studio, covering for us during our travels. He enjoys working and teaching in Japan.

The Mudarri Luna Moth stays out all night, and is attracted to the bright lights of the Ginza and loud music with a strong beat.

ride a paper crane?
I could not believe my eyes!
off to catch my own!

This design will introduce a different proportion that creates longer hindwings, and a different treatment for color change on the abdomen. It will also introduce the moth head.

The *Actias luna* (Luna) moth was the real world inspiration for this model.

Photo by Megan McCarty. (Source: *http://upload.wikimedia. org/wikipedia/commons/9/92/Male_Luna_Moth,_Megan_ McCarty141.jpg*)

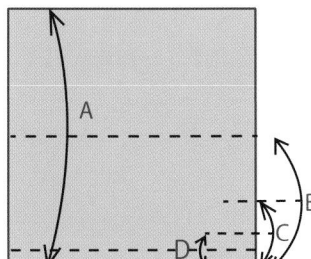

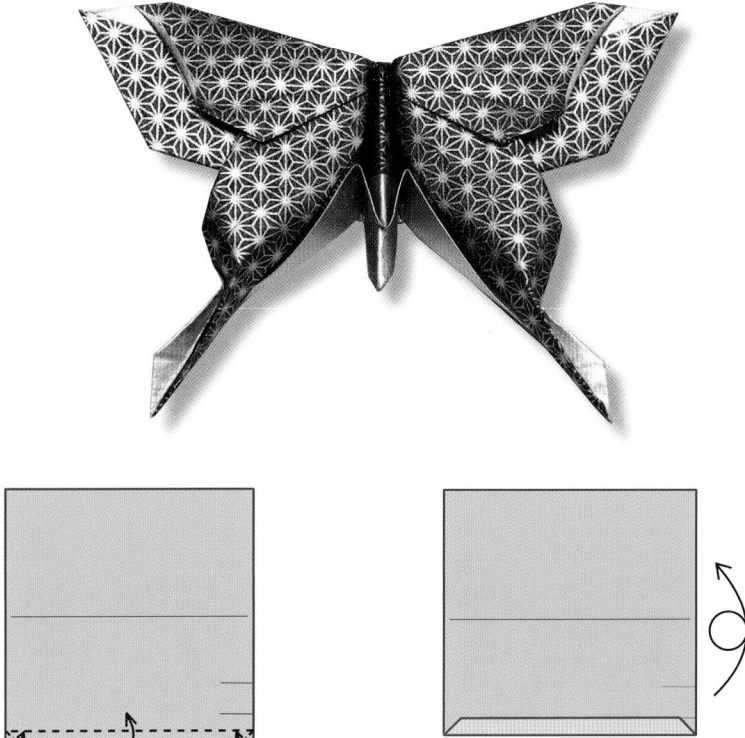

1. Begin with the major color facing up. (A) Valley-fold in half, bottom to top. Unfold. (B) Make a pinch mark halfway from the bottom edge to the valley crease above. (C) Make a pinch mark halfway from the bottom edge to pinch mark "B." (D) Valley-fold the bottom edge up to the lowest pinch mark. Unfold.

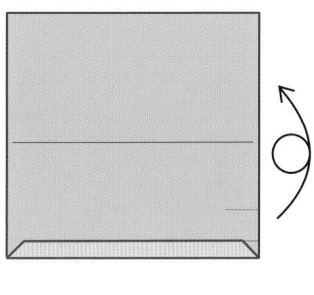

2. Valley-fold the bottom two corners to the bottom valley crease. Use the bottom valley crease to fold the bottom edge up.

3. Turn the paper over, bottom to top.

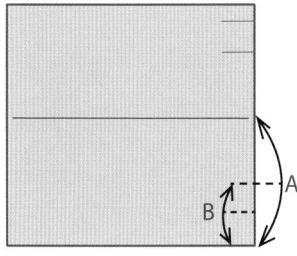

4. The folded edge should be at the top. (A) Make a pinch mark halfway from the bottom edge to the valley crease above. (B) Make a pinch mark halfway from the bottom edge to pinch mark "A."

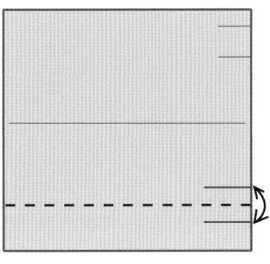

5. Lay the lower pinch mark on top of the upper pinch mark and valley-fold all the way across the paper. Unfold.

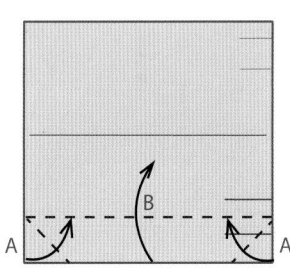

6. Valley-fold the bottom two corners to the full-length valley crease. Use the bottom valley crease to fold the bottom edge up.

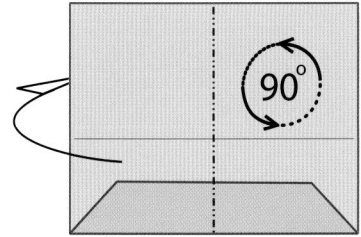

7. Mountain-fold the left half behind. Rotate 90 degrees counterclockwise.

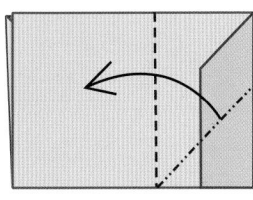

8. Squash-fold the right side.

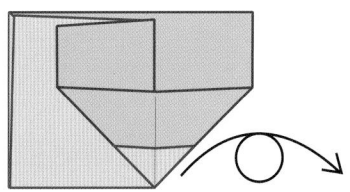

9. Your paper should look like this. Turn it over, left to right.

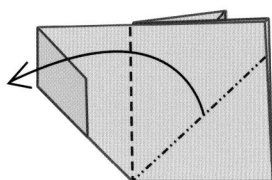

10. Squash fold.

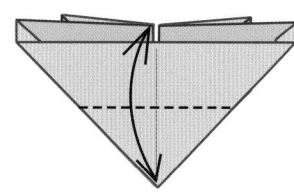

11. Valley-fold the bottom corner up to the top of the split. Unfold.

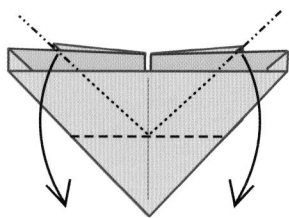

12. Squash-fold the left and right sections to form the wings.

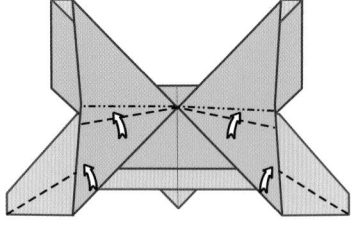

13. Crimp the middle of the top layer of each wing down, swiveling the leading edge of the hindwing up and stopping at the outer corner.

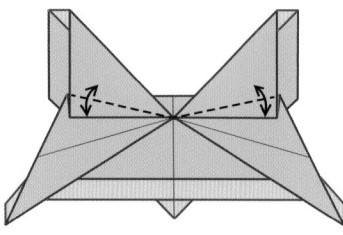

14. Valley-fold and unfold the middle folded edges.

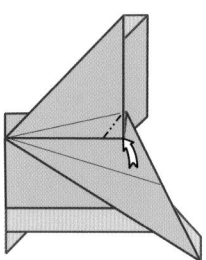

15. Inside-reverse-fold the indicated corner into the wing area and up to the crease formed in the previous step.

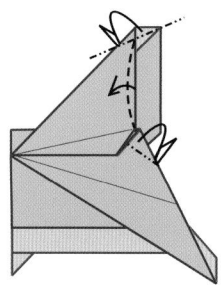

16. Mountain-fold the free corner in the middle of the wing area. Make a slightly curved valley fold along the raw edge of the forewing, forming a *lunule*.

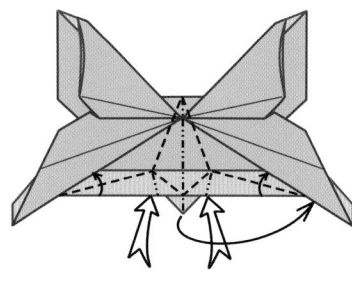

17. Begin to form the body by mountain-folding the middle and then inside-reverse-folding the bottom edges up.

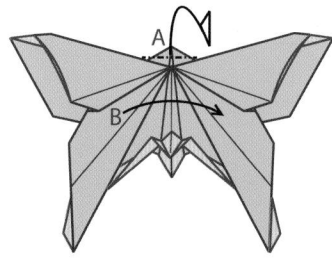

18. (A) Flatten and then mountain-fold the top corner for the head. (B) Bring the wings together with the body in between.

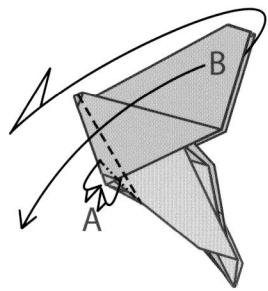

19. (A) Mountain-fold the abdomen edges inside. (B) Fold the wings down on each side.

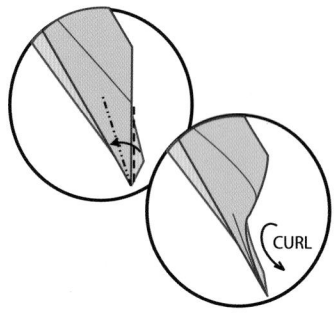

20. Valley-fold the exposed triangle of paper over the tail end of the hindwing. Mountain-fold the pointed end of the hindwing and gently curl the tail end.

The Mudarri Luna Moth.

Le Papillon de Nuit

This "butterfly of the night" is also called the "LaFosse Moth." It is more complicated than other models because it begins from a blintzed square. The "hidden" paper allows for a segmented abdomen.

> *Papillon de Nuit*
> *spirit of my grandfather*
> *has feathery ears!*

This design introduces the blintzed square, segmented abdomen, and also the moth's antennae.

The *Hyalophora cecropia* moth was the real world inspiration for this model.

Photo by Tom Peterson. (Source: *http://upload.wikimedia.org/wikipedia/commons/3/3b/Hyalophora_cecropia1.jpg*)

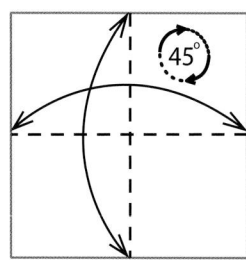

1. Begin with the minor color facing up. Valley-fold the paper in half, edge to edge both ways, unfolding after each. Rotate the paper 45 degrees.

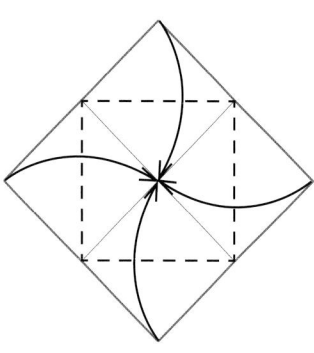

2. Valley-fold each of the four corners to meet in the middle.

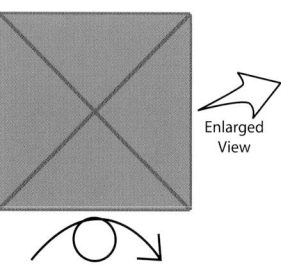

3. Turn the paper over. (Enlarged views to follow.)

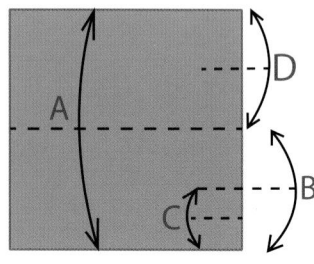

4. (A) Valley-fold bottom edge to top. Unfold. (B) Bottom edge to center crease, make a pinch mark and unfold. (C) Bottom edge to pinch mark "B," make a pinch mark and unfold. (D) Top edge to center crease, make a pinch mark and unfold.

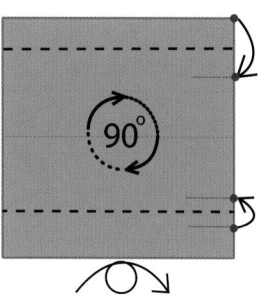

5. Top: Valley-fold the top edge to the pinch mark below it. Bottom: Lay the lowest pinch mark upon pinch mark just above it and valley-fold all the way across the paper. Rotate the paper 90 degrees counterclockwise and flip the paper top to bottom.

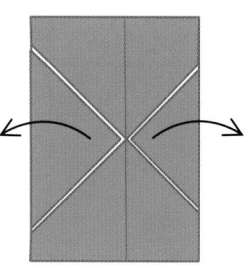

6. Open out the two triangle flaps.

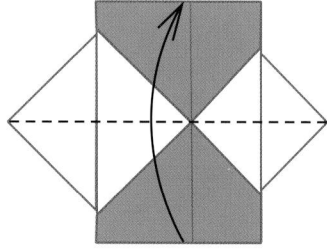

7. Valley-fold the paper in half, bottom to top.

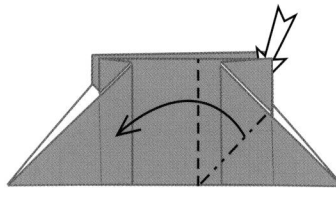

8. Squash-fold the right section.

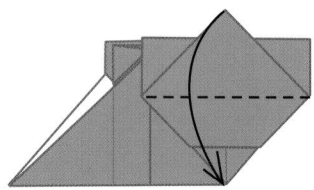

9. Valley-fold the top corner to the bottom.

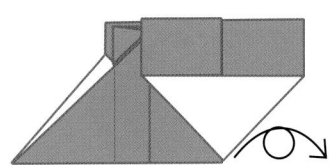

10. Your paper should look like this. Turn over, left to right.

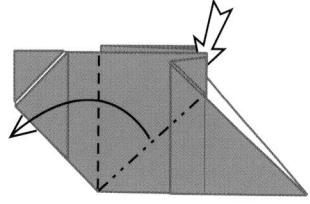

11. Squash-fold the right section.

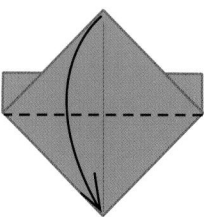

12. Valley-fold the top corner to the bottom.

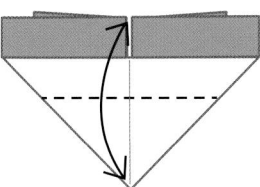

13. Valley-fold the bottom corner to the top of the split. Unfold.

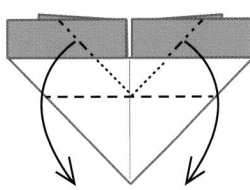

14. One at a time, squash-fold the top left and right sections to form the wings.

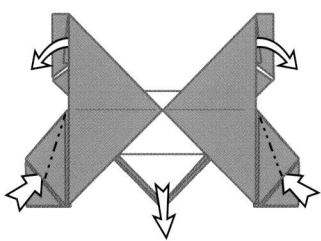

15. Pull out the hidden flaps in the forewings. Open and squash-fold the pockets in the hindwings. Pull out the triangle flap on the abdomen.

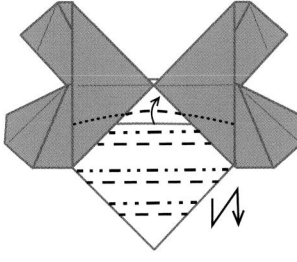

16. Mountain- and valley-fold pleats in the top layer of the abdomen. Fold up a small portion of the top layer above the abdomen.

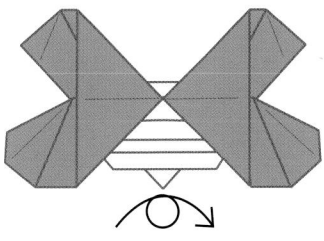

17. Your paper should look like this. Turn the model over, left to right.

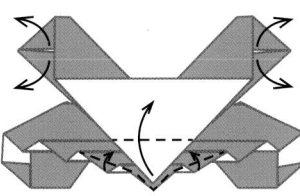

18. Pull open the top layers of the pockets in the forewings. Valley-fold the bottom corner of the center triangle flap up. Valley-fold the outside edges of the abdomen, making them trim.

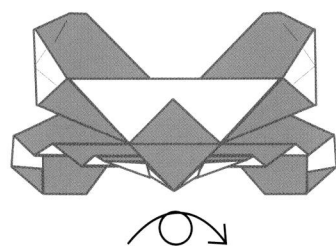

19. Your paper should look like this. Turn the model over, left to right.

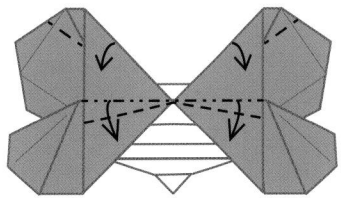

20. Roll the top layers of the forewings downward and crimp the middle area of each wing.

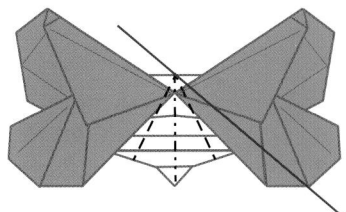

21. Mountain- and valley-fold to separate the wings from the abdomen. Open the wings out to each side of the body.

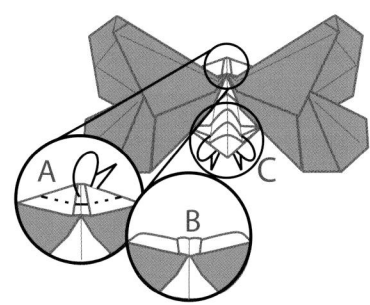

22. (A) Squash-fold the paper for the head. (B) Mountain-fold the corner behind. Leave the flanking edges visible, to simulate the large, featherlike antennae of the moth. (C) Mountain-fold the edges of the abdomen inside the model.

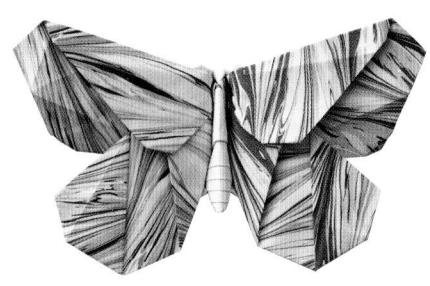

Le Papillon de Nuit.

The Tuttle Story

"Books to Span the East and West"

Many people are surprised to learn that the world's largest publisher of books on Asia had its humble beginnings in the tiny American state of Vermont. The company's founder, Charles Tuttle, came from a New England family steeped in publishing.

Tuttle's father was a noted antiquarian dealer in Rutland, Vermont. Young Charles honed his knowledge of the trade working in the family bookstore, and later in the rare books section of Columbia University Library. His passion for beautiful books—old and new—never wavered throughout his long career as a bookseller and publisher.

After graduating from Harvard, Tuttle enlisted in the military and in 1945 was sent to Tokyo to work on General Douglas MacArthur's staff. He was tasked with helping to revive the Japanese publishing industry, which had been utterly devastated by the war. When his tour of duty was completed, he left the military, married a talented and beautiful singer, Reiko Chiba, and in 1948 began several successful business ventures.

To his astonishment, Tuttle discovered that postwar Tokyo was actually a book-lover's paradise. He befriended dealers in the Kanda district and began supplying rare Japanese editions to American libraries. He also imported American books to sell to the thousands of GIs stationed in Japan. By 1949, Tuttle's business was thriving, and he opened Tokyo's very first English-language bookstore in the Takashimaya Department Store in Ginza, to great success. Two years later, he began publishing books to fulfill the growing interest of foreigners in all things Asian.

Though a Westerner, Tuttle was hugely instrumental in bringing a knowledge of Japan and Asia to a world hungry for information about the East. By the time of his death in 1993, he had published over 6,000 books on Asian culture, history and art—a legacy honored by Emperor Hirohito in 1983 with the "Order of the Sacred Treasure," the highest honor Japan can bestow upon a non-Japanese.

The Tuttle company today maintains an active backlist of some 1,500 titles, many of which have been continuously in print since the 1950s and 1960s—a great testament to Charles Tuttle's skill as a publisher. More than 60 years after its founding, Tuttle Publishing is more active today than at any time in its history, still inspired by Charles Tuttle's core mission—to publish fine books to span the East and West and provide a greater understanding of each.

Published by Tuttle Publishing, an imprint of Periplus Editions (HK) Ltd.

www.tuttlepublishing.com

Library of Congress Cataloging-in-Publication Data

LaFosse, Michael G.
 Michael LaFosse's origami butterflies : elegant designs from a master folder / by Michael G. LaFosse and Richard L. Alexander, Origamido, Inc.
     pages cm
   Includes bibliographical references.
  ISBN 978-4-8053-1226-1 (pbk.)
 1. Origami. 2. Butterflies. I. Alexander, Richard L., 1953- II. Title. III. Title: Origami butterflies.
 TT872.5.L34 2013
 736'.982--dc23
                        2012042003
 ISBN: 978-4-8053-1226-1

DISTRIBUTED BY

North America
Latin America & Europe
Tuttle Publishing
364 Innovation Drive, North Clarendon, VT 05759-9436 U.S.A.
Tel: (802) 773-8930; Fax: (802) 773-6993
info@tuttlepublishing.com; www.tuttlepublishing.com

Japan
Tuttle Publishing
Yaekari Building, 3rd Floor, 5-4-12 Osaki,
Shinagawa-ku, Tokyo 141 0032
Tel: (81) 03 5437-0171; Fax: (81) 03 5437-0755
sales@tuttle.co.jp; www.tuttle.co.jp

Asia Pacific
Berkeley Books Pte. Ltd.
61 Tai Seng Avenue #02-12, Singapore 534167
Tel: (65) 6280-1330; Fax: (65) 6280-6290
inquiries@periplus.com.sg; www.periplus.com

First edition
17 16 15 14 13   5 4 3 2

Printed in Hong Kong   1310EP

TUTTLE PUBLISHING® is a registered trademark of Tuttle Publishing, a division of Periplus Editions (HK) Ltd.